Easy Pasta

A classic kitchen collection for the busy cook

MURDOCH BOOKS

Contents

13 Ratatouille and pasta soup

7 Bean and pasta soup with sausage

14 Lamb and fusilli soup

16 Tuna, green bean and onion salad

19 Farfalle salad with spinach

Soups
and salads

Tortellini and egg soup

»PREPARATION 15 MINUTES »COOKING TIME 10 MINUTES »SERVES 2

1 Beat eggs in a small bowl with a fork. Stir in parmesan and rocket, then set aside.

2 Combine the chicken stock and 500 ml (16 fl oz/2 cups) water in a small saucepan, then bring to the boil. Add the tortellini and peas and simmer for 6–8 minutes, or until tender. Remove the pan from the heat, then transfer the tortellini and peas with a slotted spoon to a warmed serving bowl. Spoon a few tablespoons of the hot cooking liquid over the pasta to keep moist.

3 Working quickly, pour the egg mixture into the hot cooking liquid in a thin stream, stirring lightly with a fork so that the egg cooks in thin strands. Ladle the hot mixture over the pasta and the peas and scatter with extra parmesan. Season with sea salt and freshly ground black pepper and serve immediately.

2 eggs

1½ tablespoons finely grated parmesan, plus extra, to serve

1 large handful rocket (arugula), coarsely chopped

500 ml (16 fl oz/2 cups) chicken stock

120 g (5 oz/1½ cups) frozen cheese-filled tortellini

70 g (2½ oz/½ cup) frozen baby peas

Bean and pasta soup with sausage

»PREPARATION 25 MINUTES »COOKING TIME 40 MINUTES »SERVES 4–6

1 Chop the Italian sausages into small pieces. Heat the oil in a large heavy-based saucepan and add the sausage pieces. Cook over medium heat for 5 minutes, or until golden, stirring regularly. Remove from the pan, then set aside and drain on paper towel.

2 Add the leek, garlic, carrot and celery to the saucepan and cook for 2–3 minutes, or until soft, stirring occasionally. Add the flour and stir for 1 minute. Gradually stir in the combined stock cubes, water and wine. Bring to the boil, reduce the heat and simmer for 10 minutes.

3 Add the pasta and beans to the pan. Increase the heat and cook for 8–10 minutes, or until the pasta is al dente. Return the sausage to the pan and season to taste. Serve with chopped fresh parsley, if desired.

Note Use dried beans, if preferred. Put the beans in a bowl, cover with water and leave to soak overnight. Drain the beans and add to a large saucepan with enough water to cover well. Bring to the boil, then reduce the heat and simmer for 1 hour. Drain well before adding to the soup.

4 Italian sausages
2 teaspoons olive oil
2 leeks, white part only, sliced
1 garlic clove, crushed
1 large carrot, cut into small cubes
2 celery stalks, sliced
2 tablespoons plain (all-purpose) flour
2 beef stock (bouillon) cubes, crumbled
2 litres (70 fl oz/8 cups) boiling water
125 ml (4 fl oz/½ cup) white wine
125 g (4½ oz) conchiglie (shell pasta)
440 g (15½ oz) tinned mixed beans, drained
chopped parsley, to serve (optional)

Ravioli soup

1 Leaving the root end attached, slice the leek lengthways a few times. Wash thoroughly to remove any grit, then drain. Chop into small pieces, discarding the root.

2 Wash the silverbeet leaves and cut away the thick white stems. Tear the leaves into smaller pieces. Set aside.

3 Put the leek, carrot, zucchini and celery in the slow cooker. Add the mushrooms, then pour in the stock and soy sauce. Cook on high for 3–4 hours, until the vegetables are cooked. About 30 minutes before the end of cooking time, add the silverbeet and ravioli. Cover and

cook for a further 20 minutes until the pasta is al dente.

4 Using kitchen tongs, remove the mushrooms, discard the stems, then thinly slice the mushroom caps and return them to the soup. Ladle the soup and pasta into serving bowls and sprinkle with freshly ground black pepper.

Note This recipe is for a slow-cooker appliance. It can also be made in a pan on the cooktop. At step 3, simmer vegetables in stock until tender. Add silverbeet and ravioli 10 minutes before the end of the cooking time.

1 small leek, white part only
3 silverbeet (Swiss chard) leaves
1 carrot, diced
1 zucchini (courgette), diced
1 celery stalk, including some leaves, diced
2 whole dried Chinese mushrooms
1.5 litres (52 fl oz/6 cups) chicken stock
1 tablespoon light soy sauce
250 g (9 oz) fresh ravioli pasta, such as chicken and mushroom

Spicy chicken broth with pasta

»PREPARATION 1 HOUR »COOKING TIME 50 MINUTES »SERVES 4

1 Put the chicken pieces, carrot, celery and leek in a large heavy-based saucepan. Push the chicken pieces to one side and add the egg whites to the vegetables. Using a wire whisk, beat for a minute or so, until frothy (take care not to use a pan that can be scratched by the whisk).

2 Warm the stock in a separate saucepan, then gradually add the stock to the first pan, whisking continuously to froth the egg whites. Continue whisking while slowly bringing to the boil. Make a hole in the froth on top with a spoon and leave to simmer for 30 minutes, without stirring.

3 Line a large strainer with a damp tea towel (dish towel) or double thickness of muslin (cheesecloth) and strain the broth into a clean bowl (discard the chicken pieces and vegetables). Season with salt, pepper and Tabasco sauce. Set aside until you are ready to serve.

4 To make the coriander pasta, sift the flour into a bowl and make a well in the centre. Whisk the egg and oil together and pour into the well. Mix together to make a soft pasta dough and knead on a lightly floured surface for 2 minutes, or until smooth.

5 Divide the pasta dough into four even portions. Roll one portion out very thinly and cover with a layer of evenly spaced coriander leaves. Roll out another portion of pasta and lay this on top of the leaves, then gently roll the layers together. Repeat with the remaining pasta and coriander.

6 Cut out squares of pasta around the leaves. The pasta may then be left to sit and dry out if it is not needed immediately. When you are ready to serve, heat the chicken broth gently in a pan. As the broth simmers, add the pasta and cook for 1 minute. Serve immediately.

Note The egg whites added to the vegetable and chicken stock make the broth very clear, rather than leaving it with the normal cloudy appearance of chicken stock. This is called clarifying the stock. When you strain the broth through a tea towel or muslin, don't press the solids to extract the extra liquid or the broth will become cloudy. It is necessary to make a hole in the froth on top to prevent the stock boiling over.

350 g (12 oz) chicken thighs or wings, skin removed
2 carrots, finely chopped
2 celery stalks, finely chopped
2 small leeks, white part only, finely chopped
3 egg whites
1.5 litres (52 fl oz/6 cups) chicken stock
Tabasco sauce

Coriander pasta
60 g (2¼ oz/½ cup) plain (all-purpose) flour
1 egg
½ teaspoon sesame oil
90 g (3¼ oz) coriander (cilantro) leaves

Minestrone

with pesto

1 Soak the borlotti beans in plenty of cold water overnight. Drain and rinse thoroughly under cold water.

2 Heat the olive oil in a large, deep saucepan over low heat. Add the onion, garlic and pancetta and cook, stirring occasionally, for 8–10 minutes, or until softened. Add the celery, carrot and potato and cook for 5 minutes. Stir in the tomato paste, tomatoes, basil and drained borlotti beans. Season with freshly ground black pepper. Add the stock and bring slowly to the boil. Cover and simmer, stirring occasionally, for 1½ hours.

3 Add the zucchini, peas, green beans, silverbeet, parsley and the pasta. Simmer for 8–10 minutes, or until the vegetables and pasta are al dente. Check for seasoning and adjust if necessary.

4 To make the pesto, combine the basil, pine nuts and garlic with a pinch of salt in a food processor. Process until finely chopped. With the motor running, slowly add the olive oil. Transfer to a bowl and stir in the parmesan and some ground black pepper to taste. Serve with the soup.

Note Toast the pine nuts in a dry frying pan over medium heat, stirring constantly, until they are golden brown and fragrant. Watch carefully as they will burn easily.

125 g (4½ oz) dried borlotti (cranberry) beans
60 ml (2 fl oz/¼ cup) olive oil
1 large onion, finely chopped
2 garlic cloves, crushed
60 g (2¼ oz) pancetta, finely chopped
1 celery stalk, halved lengthways and cut into thin slices
1 carrot, halved lengthways and cut into thin slices
1 potato, diced
2 teaspoons tomato paste (concentrated purée)
400 g (14 oz) tinned crushed tomatoes
6 basil leaves, roughly torn
2 litres (70 fl oz/8 cups) chicken or vegetable stock
2 zucchini (courgettes), cut into thin slices
115 g (4 oz/¾ cup) fresh peas, shelled
60 g (2¼ oz) green beans, cut into short lengths
90 g (3 oz) silverbeet (Swiss chard) leaves, shredded
3 tablespoons chopped flat-leaf (Italian) parsley
70 g (2½ oz) ditalini or other small pasta

Pesto
3 handfuls basil leaves
20 g (¾ oz) lightly toasted pine nuts (see Note)
2 garlic cloves
100 ml (3½ fl oz) olive oil
25 g (1 oz/¼ cup) freshly grated parmesan cheese

Lemon-scented broth with tortellini

»PREPARATION 10 MINUTES »COOKING TIME 20 MINUTES »SERVES 4–6

1 Using a vegetable peeler, peel wide strips from the lemon. Remove the white pith with a small sharp knife. Cut three of the wide pieces of lemon zest into fine strips and set aside for garnishing.

2 Combine the wide lemon strips, white wine, consommé and 750 ml (26 fl oz/3 cups) water in a large saucepan. Cook for 10 minutes over low heat. Remove the lemon zest from the pan and bring the mixture to the boil. Add the pasta and parsley and season with black pepper. Cook for 6–7 minutes, or until the pasta is al dente. Garnish with fine strips of lemon zest and grated parmesan cheese.

1 lemon

125 ml (4 fl oz/½ cup) white wine

440 g (15½ oz) tinned chicken consommé

375 g (13 oz) fresh or dried veal or chicken tortellini

4 tablespoons chopped flat-leaf (Italian) parsley

grated parmesan cheese, to serve

Ratatouille and pasta soup

»PREPARATION 25 MINUTES »COOKING TIME 40 MINUTES »SERVES 6

1 Chop 1 eggplant (aubergine). To remove any bitterness, spread the eggplant pieces out in a colander and sprinkle generously with salt. Set aside for 20 minutes and then rinse thoroughly and pat dry with paper towels.

2 Chop 1 large onion, 1 large red and 1 large green capsicum (pepper), and slice 3 zucchini (courgettes). Heat 2 tablespoons olive oil in a large heavy-based saucepan and cook the onion over medium heat for 10 minutes, or until soft and lightly golden. Add the capsicum, zucchini, eggplant and 2 crushed garlic cloves and stir-fry for 5 minutes.

3 Add 800 g (1 lb 12 oz) tinned crushed tomatoes, 1 teaspoon dried oregano leaves, ½ teaspoon dried thyme leaves and 1 litre (35 fl oz/ 4 cups) vegetable stock. Bring to the boil, reduce the heat and simmer for 10 minutes, or until the vegetables are tender. Add 50 g (1¾ oz) fusilli and cook for a further 15 minutes, or until the fusilli is tender. Serve with shavings of fresh parmesan cheese scattered on top.

Lamb and fusilli soup

» PREPARATION 25 MINUTES » COOKING TIME 40 MINUTES » SERVES 6–8

1 Heat the oil in a large saucepan. Cook the cubed lamb, in batches, until golden brown. Remove each batch as it is done and drain on paper towel. Set aside.

2 Add the onion to the pan and cook for 2 minutes or until softened. Return the meat to the pan, add the carrot, celery, tomato and stock. Stir to combine and bring to the boil. Reduce the heat to low and simmer, covered, for 15 minutes. Add the fusilli and stir to prevent the pasta from sticking to the pan. Simmer, uncovered, for 10 minutes, until the lamb and pasta are tender. Sprinkle with parsley before serving.

2 tablespoons oil

500 g (1 lb 2 oz) lean lamb meat, cubed

2 onions, finely chopped

2 carrots, diced

4 celery stalks, diced

425 g (15 oz) tinned crushed tomatoes

2 litres (70 fl oz/8 cups) beef stock

500 g (1 lb 2 oz) fusilli

chopped flat-leaf (Italian) parsley, to serve

Chargrilled squid and pasta salad

»PREPARATION 15 MINUTES »COOKING TIME 15 MINUTES »SERVES 4

1 Cook 320 g (11¼ oz) linguine in a saucepan of boiling, salted water for 12 minutes or according to the packet instructions until al dente. Drain, then cool under cold water and drain again.

2 Finely dice 4 tomatoes and shred 1 head of radicchio. Combine the tomatoes, radicchio, 1 handful each of flat-leaf (Italian) parsley leaves and basil leaves, and 115 g (4 oz/⅔ cup) small black olives in a bowl. Add the pasta and toss to combine.

3 Lightly whisk together 4 finely chopped anchovy fillets, 2 crushed garlic cloves, 2 tablespoons lemon juice and 6 tablespoons olive oil. Drizzle over the pasta salad.

4 Cut open 500 g (1 lb 2 oz) cleaned squid tubes and tentacles and finely score the insides with a small, sharp knife. Heat a chargrill pan over high heat or a barbecue to high. Cook the squid tubes and tentacles for 3 minutes, turning once, or until lightly charred and cooked through. Add to the salad, toss well to combine and serve immediately with lemon wedges.

Tuna, green bean and onion salad

» PREPARATION 20 MINUTES   » COOKING TIME 15 MINUTES   » SERVES 4

1 Cook the chopped beans in a large saucepan of boiling water for 1–2 minutes, until tender but still crisp. Remove with a slotted spoon and rinse under cold water. Drain the beans and transfer to a bowl.

2 Cook the pasta in a saucepan of boiling salted water until al dente. Drain, rinse under cold water and drain again. Add to the beans.

3 Heat half the oil in a frying pan. Add the tuna and onion and gently sauté until the tuna is just cooked through. Stir the tuna carefully to prevent it from breaking up. Add the vinegar, increase the heat to high and briefly cook until the dressing has reduced and lightly coats the tuna. Transfer the tuna and onion to a bowl.

4 Toss the beans, pasta, tuna and onion together and mix with the remaining olive oil. Season to taste. Allow to cool before serving.

200 g (7 oz) green beans, trimmed and cut into short lengths
300 g (10½ oz) penne rigate
125 ml (4 fl oz/½ cup) olive oil
250 g (9 oz) tuna steak, cut into thick slices
1 red onion, thinly sliced
1 tablespoon balsamic vinegar

Tuscan warm pasta salad

»PREPARATION 15 MINUTES   »COOKING TIME 15 MINUTES   »SERVES 6

1 Add the rigatoni to a large saucepan of rapidly boiling water and cook until al dente. Drain the pasta thoroughly and transfer to a large bowl.

2 While the pasta is cooking, whisk together the oil, garlic and vinegar. Toss the dressing through the hot pasta, then allow the pasta to cool slightly. Add the artichoke hearts, prosciutto, sun-dried tomato, basil, rocket, pine nuts and olives.

3 Toss all the ingredients together until well combined. Season to taste.

Note To toast the pine nuts, cook in a dry frying pan over medium heat for 1–2 minutes, until lightly golden. Allow to cool.

500 g (1 lb 2 oz) rigatoni
80 ml (2½ fl oz/⅓ cup) olive oil
1 garlic clove, crushed
1 tablespoon balsamic vinegar
425 g (15 oz) tinned artichoke hearts, drained and quartered
8 thin prosciutto slices, chopped
80 g (2¾ oz/½ cup) sun-dried tomatoes in oil, drained and thinly sliced
15 g (½ oz/¼ cup) basil, shredded
70 g (2½ oz) rocket (arugula) leaves, washed and drained well
40 g (1½ oz/¼ cup) pine nuts, toasted
45 g (1½ oz/¼ cup) black Italian olives

Linguine salad with olives and basil

»PREPARATION 20 MINUTES »COOKING TIME 15 MINUTES »SERVES 4–6

1 Cook the linguine in a large saucepan of salted, boiling water according to packet instructions or until al dente. Drain well in a colander, then combine in a large bowl with 1 tablespoon of the olive oil. Set aside.

2 Heat 1 tablespoon of the oil in a large frying pan over medium heat. Add the onion and cook, stirring, for 2–3 minutes or until starting to soften, then add the olives, lemon rind and juice and stir until well combined. Add to the pasta.

3 Wipe the frying pan clean and heat the remaining olive oil over medium–high heat. Add the garlic and cook for 30 seconds or until golden. Add the breadcrumbs and cook, stirring often, for 3 minutes, or until crumbs are golden. Remove from the heat and stir in the parsley.

4 Add the basil and radicchio to the pasta mixture in the bowl, then season well with sea salt and freshly ground black pepper. Toss well. Divide the salad among bowls. Drizzle with extra virgin olive oil, sprinkle with the garlic crumbs and garnish with the basil leaves. Serve immediately with a little tapénade, if using.

400 g (14 oz) linguine pasta
60 ml (2 fl oz/¼ cup) extra virgin olive oil, plus extra, to serve
2 small red onions, peeled and thinly sliced
95 g (3¼ oz/½ cup) chopped pitted kalamata olives
2 teaspoons finely grated lemon rind
60 ml (2 fl oz/¼ cup) lemon juice
2 garlic cloves, crushed
80 g (2¾ oz/1 cup) coarse breadcrumbs, made from day-old bread
2 tablespoons flat-leaf (Italian) parsley, coarsely chopped
1 large handful basil, thinly sliced, reserving 12 leaves to garnish
2 small or ½ large head of radicchio, leaves trimmed and thinly sliced
purchased tapénade (olive paste), to serve (optional)

Farfalle salad with spinach

»PREPARATION 20 MINUTES »COOKING TIME 15 MINUTES »SERVES 6

1 Cook the pasta in a large saucepan of rapidly boiling salted water until al dente. Drain, rinse under cold water and drain again. Allow to cool, then transfer to a large salad bowl.

2 Trim the spring onions and thinly slice diagonally. Add to the pasta with the tomato, spinach, pine nuts and oregano.

3 To make the dressing, combine the olive oil, chilli, garlic and some salt and pepper in a small screw-top jar and shake well. Pour the dressing over the top of the salad and toss well to combine.

500 g (1 lb 2 oz) farfalle or spiral pasta
3 spring onions (scallions)
50 g (1¾ oz) sun-dried tomatoes, cut into strips
1 kg (2 lb 4 oz) English spinach, stalks trimmed and leaves shredded
50 g (1¾ oz/⅓ cup) pine nuts, toasted
1 tablespoon chopped oregano
60 ml (2 fl oz/¼ cup) olive oil
1 teaspoon sliced chilli
1 garlic clove, crushed

24 Tortellini with eggplant

25 Pumpkin and herb ravioli

28 Ravioli with zucchini and pine nuts

29 Ricotta tortellini with silverbeet

31 Ravioli with herbs

Filled and baked pasta meals

Herb-filled ravioli with sage butter

»PREPARATION 1 HOUR »COOKING TIME 10 MINUTES »SERVES 4

1 To make the pasta, sift the flour into a bowl and make a well in the centre. Gradually mix in the eggs and olive oil. Turn the dough out onto a lightly floured surface and knead for 6 minutes, until smooth. Cover with plastic wrap and leave for 30 minutes.

2 To make the filling, mix together the ricotta cheese, parmesan and herbs. Season.

3 Divide the dough into four even portions. Lightly flour a large work surface and, using a floured rolling pin, roll out one portion from the centre to the edge. Continue rolling, always rolling from in front of you outwards. Rotate the dough often. Fold the dough in half and then roll it out again. Continue this process seven times to make a smooth circle about 5 mm (¼ inch) thick. Roll out the sheet quickly and smoothly to a thickness of 2.5 mm (⅛ inch). Make four sheets of pasta, two slightly larger than the others. Cover with a tea towel (dish towel).

4 Spread one of the smaller pasta sheets out on a work surface and place heaped teaspoons of filling at 5 cm (2 inch) intervals. Brush a little water between the filling along the cutting lines. Place one of the larger sheets on top and firmly press the sheets together along the cutting lines. Cut the ravioli with a pastry wheel or sharp knife and transfer to a lightly floured tray. Repeat with the remaining dough and filling.

5 To make the sage butter, melt the butter in a small heavy-based saucepan over low heat, without stirring or shaking. Carefully pour the clear butter into a container and discard the white sediment. Return the clarified butter to a clean pan and heat gently over medium heat. Add the sage leaves and cook until crisp but not brown. Remove and drain on paper towels. Reserve the warm butter.

6 Cook the ravioli in batches in a large saucepan of salted simmering water for 5–6 minutes, until tender. Top with the warm sage butter and leaves. Garnish with parmesan cheese shavings.

Note Don't cook the ravioli in rapidly boiling water or the squares will split and lose the filling.

Pasta
300 g (10½ oz) plain (all-purpose) flour
3 eggs, beaten
60 ml (2 fl oz/¼ cup) olive oil

Filling
250 g (9 oz/1 cup) ricotta cheese
2 tablespoons freshly grated parmesan cheese, plus extra, shaved, to garnish
2 teaspoons snipped chives
1 tablespoon chopped flat-leaf (Italian) parsley
2 teaspoons chopped basil
1 teaspoon chopped thyme

Sage butter
200 g (7 oz) butter
12 sage leaves

Giant conchiglie with ricotta and rocket

»PREPARATION 50 MINUTES »COOKING TIME 1 HOUR »SERVES 6

1 Cook the giant conchiglie in a large saucepan of rapidly boiling salted water until al dente. Drain and arrange the shells on two non-stick baking trays to prevent them sticking together. Cover lightly with plastic wrap.

2 To make the filling, combine all the ingredients in a large bowl. Spoon the filling into the shells, taking care not to overfill them or they will split.

3 To make the cheese sauce, melt the butter in a small saucepan over low heat. Add the flour and cook, stirring, for 1 minute, until golden and smooth. Remove the pan from the heat and gradually stir in the milk. Return to the heat and stir constantly until the sauce boils and begins to thicken. Simmer for a further minute. Remove from the heat and stir in the gruyère cheese with the basil and season to taste.

4 Preheat the oven to 180°C (350°F/Gas 4). Spread about 250 ml (9 fl oz/1 cup) of the cheese sauce over the base of a 3 litre (104 fl oz/ 12 cup) capacity ovenproof dish. Arrange the filled conchiglie over the sauce, top with the remaining sauce and bake for 30 minutes, or until the sauce is golden.

5 Pour the bottled pasta sauce into a saucepan and add the chopped oregano. Cook over medium heat for 5 minutes, until heated through. To serve, divide the pasta sauce among the warmed serving plates, top with the conchiglie and sprinkle with the basil leaves.

40 giant conchiglie (shell pasta)

Filling
500 g (1 lb 2 oz) ricotta cheese
100 g (3½ oz/1 cup) grated parmesan cheese
150 g (5½ oz) rocket (arugula), finely shredded
1 egg, lightly beaten
185 g (6½ oz) marinated globe artichokes, finely chopped
80 g (2¾ oz) sun-dried tomatoes, finely chopped
95 g (3¼ oz) sun-dried capsicum (pepper), finely chopped

Cheese sauce
60 g (2¼ oz) butter
30 g (1 oz/¼ cup) plain (all-purpose) flour
750 ml (26 fl oz/3 cups) milk
100 g (3½ oz) gruyère cheese, grated
2 tablespoons chopped basil

600 ml (21 fl oz) bottled pasta sauce
2 tablespoons oregano, chopped
2 tablespoons basil

Tortellini with eggplant

» PREPARATION 10 MINUTES » COOKING TIME 20 MINUTES » SERVES 4

1 Cut the red capsicum in half, remove the seeds and membrane and cut into small squares. Cut the eggplant into small cubes.

2 Cook the fresh tortellini in a large saucepan of rapidly boiling salted water until al dente. Drain and return to the pan.

3 While the pasta is cooking, heat the oil in a large frying pan, add the garlic and capsicum and stir over medium heat for 1 minute.

Add the eggplant to the pan and cook, stirring gently, for 5 minutes, or until lightly browned.

4 Stir in the undrained tomatoes and stock. Bring to the boil, then reduce the heat to low, cover the pan and cook for 10 minutes, or until the vegetables are tender. Add the basil and pasta and stir until mixed through.

Note Cut the eggplant just before using, as it turns brown when it is exposed to the air.

1 red capsicum (pepper)
500 g (1 lb 2 oz) eggplant (aubergine)
500 g (1 lb 2 oz) fresh cheese and spinach tortellini
60 ml (2 fl oz/¼ cup) oil
2 garlic cloves, crushed
425 g (15 oz) tinned crushed tomatoes
250 ml (9 fl oz/1 cup) vegetable stock
25 g (1 oz) chopped basil

Pumpkin and herb ravioli

»PREPARATION 50 MINUTES »COOKING TIME 1 HOUR 15 MINUTES »SERVES 6

1 Preheat the oven to 180°C (350°F/Gas 4). Place the pumpkin on an oiled baking tray and bake for 1 hour or until tender, then allow to cool. Remove the skin.

2 Place the flour and eggs in a food processor. Process for 30 seconds, or until the mixture forms a dough. Transfer to a lightly floured surface and knead for 3 minutes, until the dough is smooth and elastic. Cover with a clean cloth and set aside for 30 minutes.

3 Place the pumpkin in a bowl with the nutmeg and mash with a fork.

4 Roll out half the dough to form a rectangle about 2 mm (1/16 inch) thick. Roll out the remaining half to form a rectangle slightly larger than the first.

5 On the first rectangle of dough, place heaped teaspoonsful of the pumpkin mixture in straight rows, at intervals about 5 cm (2 inches) apart. Flatten each pumpkin mound slightly; place a sage or parsley leaf on top of each pumpkin mound.

6 Brush lightly between the filling mounds with water. Place the other sheet of dough on top and press down gently between the pumpkin mounds to seal. Cut into squares with a knife or a fluted cutter. Bring a large saucepan of water to the boil and drop in the ravioli a few at a time. Cook for 4 minutes, or until just tender. Drain well. Serve the ravioli sprinkled with salt and pepper and tossed with the melted butter and grated parmesan cheese.

Note Ravioli can be made several hours in advance. Refrigerate in layers between sheets of baking paper to prevent them sticking. Cook just before serving.

500 g (1 lb 2 oz) pumpkin (winter squash), peeled and cut into chunks
220 g (7¾ oz/1¾ cups) plain (all-purpose) flour
3 eggs, lightly beaten
¼ teaspoon freshly grated nutmeg
15 sage leaves
15 flat-leaf (Italian) parsley leaves
125 g (4½ oz) butter, melted
60 g (2¼ oz) freshly grated parmesan cheese

Ricotta-filled ravioli with fresh tomato sauce

»PREPARATION 35 MINUTES »COOKING TIME 45–50 MINUTES »SERVES 4–6

1 To make the ravioli dough, sift the flour into a bowl. Make a well in the centre, add the egg, oil and 1 teaspoon water and gradually incorporate into the flour. Turn out onto a lightly floured board, knead until smooth and elastic. Cover; set aside for 30 minutes. While the pastry is resting, make the filling and the tomato sauce.

2 To make the filling, combine all the ingredients and mix well.

3 To make the sauce, score a cross in the base of each tomato. Put in a heatproof bowl and cover with boiling water. Leave for 30 seconds, transfer to cold water, drain and peel away the skin from the cross. Cut the tomatoes in half, scoop out the seeds and chop the flesh. Chop the onion and the carrot.

4 Heat the olive oil in a large heavy-based saucepan. Add the onion, carrot and garlic. Cook gently for 5–7 minutes. Add the tomato, tomato paste, sugar, stock, worcestershire sauce and basil. Bring to the boil, reduce the heat, cover and simmer for 30 minutes. Cool slightly, then briefly process the mixture in a food processor. Keep warm.

5 Halve the ravioli dough and reshape each piece into a smooth ball. Roll out each thinly to a long oblong shape. Place teaspoons of filling in mounds at 5 cm (2 inch) intervals in regular lines on one sheet of dough. Lightly brush between the mounds with water and carefully place the other sheet of dough over the top. Press down between the filling to seal. Use a pastry wheel or knife to cut the ravioli into squares.

6 Drop the ravioli into a large saucepan of boiling water and cook for 8–10 minutes, or until tender. Remove the ravioli using a slotted spoon and place in a heated dish. Spoon over the sauce, garnish with basil leaves and serve.

Ravioli dough
125 g (4½ oz/1 cup) plain (all-purpose) flour
1 egg
1 tablespoon oil

Filling
250 g (9 oz/1 cup) ricotta cheese
½ tablespoon chopped flat-leaf (Italian) parsley
1 egg yolk

Tomato sauce
1 kg (2 lb 4 oz) ripe tomatoes
1 onion
1 carrot
1 tablespoon olive oil
2 garlic cloves, crushed
50 g (1¾ oz) tomato paste (concentrated purée)
1 teaspoon soft brown sugar
125 ml (4 fl oz/½ cup) vegetable stock
1 tablespoon worcestershire sauce
30 g (1 oz) chopped basil
basil, extra, to garnish

Ravioli with zucchini and pine nuts

»PREPARATION 5 MINUTES   »COOKING TIME 15 MINUTES   »SERVES 2

1 Bring a saucepan of salted water to the boil. Add the ravioli and cook according to the packet instructions. Drain and set aside.

2 Meanwhile, melt the butter in a small frying pan over medium heat. Add the bacon, pine nuts and sage and cook for 2 minutes, or until the bacon is crispy. Add the zucchini and lemon juice and cook, tossing occasionally, until the liquid has evaporated. Add the ravioli to the pan, add the spinach and toss until well combined. Season to taste with sea salt and freshly ground black pepper and sprinkle with the shaved parmesan. Serve immediately.

300 g (10½ oz) ready-made fresh chicken ravioli
40 g (1½ oz) butter
2 bacon slices, cut widthways into thin strips
2 tablespoons pine nuts
12 sage leaves, torn
2 zucchini (courgettes), trimmed and thinly sliced
2 tablespoons lemon juice
2 small handfuls baby spinach leaves
shaved parmesan, to serve

Ricotta tortellini with silverbeet

»PREPARATION 15 MINUTES »COOKING TIME 30 MINUTES »SERVES 4

1 Bring a large saucepan of salted water to the boil. Add the tortellini and cook according to the packet instructions or until al dente. Drain the pasta and set aside in a bowl. Gently toss ½ tablespoon of the olive oil through the pasta to stop it sticking together.

2 Heat the remaining oil in the same pan, add the onion and sauté over medium heat for 5 minutes, or until softened. Add the garlic, silverbeet and nutmeg and cook for a further 3–4 minutes, until the silverbeet has wilted.

3 Pour in the cream and bring to the boil, then reduce the heat to a simmer and cook for 3–4 minutes, or until the liquid has reduced by half. Return the tortellini to the pan, add the capers and lemon juice and gently toss to combine well.

4 Season to taste with sea salt and freshly ground black pepper, scatter the chopped tomato and grated parmesan over and serve.

500 g (1 lb 2 oz) fresh ricotta ravioli or ricotta tortellini
2½ tablespoons olive oil
1 small onion, finely chopped
1 garlic clove, crushed
400 g (14 oz/½ bunch) silverbeet (Swiss chard), stems removed, leaves washed, dried and thinly sliced
a large pinch of freshly grated nutmeg
250 ml (9 fl oz/1 cup) cream
2 tablespoons capers, rinsed and drained
2 tablespoons lemon juice
1 tomato, seeded and finely chopped
35 g (1¼ oz/⅓ cup) grated parmesan cheese

Chicken ravioli with burnt butter

»PREPARATION 25 MINUTES »COOKING TIME 10 MINUTES »SERVES 4

1 Combine the chicken, currants, pine nuts, anchovies and herbs in a bowl and season with sea salt and freshly ground black pepper. Stir to mix well.

2 Lay half the won ton wrappers on a baking paper-lined baking tray, then place about 1 tablespoon of the filling on the centre of each wrapper, flattening slightly. Lightly brush the edge of each wrapper with water to dampen, then place the remaining wrappers on top of each, pressing down the edges to seal.

3 To make the lemon burnt butter, melt the butter in a small saucepan over medium–low heat, then cook for 1 minute, until the butter and its solids begin to turn golden brown. Remove from the heat and add the lemon zest and juice.

4 Bring a large saucepan of water to the boil, add the ravioli and cook for 5 minutes, until cooked through. Drain well.

5 Place the ravioli onto a serving plate, drizzle with the lemon burnt butter, sprinkle with pine nuts and oregano, and serve immediately.

400 g (14 oz) minced (ground) chicken
50 g (1¾ oz/⅓ cup) currants
50 g (1¾ oz/⅓ cup) toasted pine nuts, plus extra, to serve
6–8 anchovy fillets, finely chopped
4 tablespoons finely chopped parsley
1 tablespoon finely chopped rosemary
1 tablespoon finely chopped oregano, plus a few leaves extra, to serve
32 won ton wrappers

Lemon burnt butter
60 g (2¼ oz) butter
1 lemon, zested
1–2 tablespoons lemon juice

Ravioli with herbs

»PREPARATION 15 MINUTES »COOKING TIME 5 MINUTES »SERVES 6

1 Combine the oil and garlic in a small bowl, then set aside. Add the ravioli to a large saucepan of rapidly boiling salted water and cook until al dente.

2 Drain the ravioli in a colander and return to the pan. Add the oil to the pasta, discarding the garlic. Add the butter and herbs to the ravioli, toss well and season. Sprinkle with parmesan to serve.

Note As a variation, use coriander (cilantro) instead of parsley.

2 tablespoons olive oil
1 garlic clove, halved
800 g (1 lb 12 oz) ricotta-filled ravioli
60 g (2¼ oz) butter, chopped
2 tablespoons chopped flat-leaf (Italian) parsley
20 g (¾ oz) chopped basil
2 tablespoons snipped chives
freshly grated parmesan cheese, to serve (optional)

Chicken ravioli with fresh tomato sauce

»PREPARATION 40 MINUTES »COOKING TIME 30 MINUTES »SERVES 4

1 Heat the oil in a medium saucepan and add the onion and garlic. Cook for 2–3 minutes, then stir in the tomato paste, wine, stock and tomato. Simmer over low heat for 20 minutes. Stir in the basil and season, to taste.

2 Meanwhile, to make the ravioli, combine chicken, basil, parmesan, spring onion, ricotta and some salt and pepper. Lay half the wrappers on a flat surface and brush with a little water. Place slightly heaped teaspoons of mixture in the centre of each wrapper. Place remaining wrappers on top and press the edges firmly together.

3 Bring a large saucepan of water to the boil and cook the ravioli a few at a time for 2–3 minutes, or until tender. Drain well. Serve with the tomato sauce and freshly grated parmesan cheese

1 tablespoon oil
1 large onion, chopped
2 garlic cloves, crushed
90 g (3¼ oz/⅓ cup) tomato paste (concentrated purée)
60 ml (2 fl oz/¼ cup) red wine
170 ml (5½ fl oz/⅔ cup) chicken stock
2 very ripe tomatoes, chopped
1 tablespoon chopped basil
freshly grated parmesan cheese, to serve

Ravioli

200 g (7 oz) minced (ground) chicken
1 tablespoon chopped basil
25 g (1 oz/¼ cup) grated parmesan cheese
3 spring onions (scallions), finely chopped
50 g (1¾ oz) fresh ricotta cheese
250 g (9 oz) packet (48) gow gee wrappers

Tortellini with mushroom sauce

»PREPARATION 15 MINUTES »COOKING TIME 10 MINUTES »SERVES 4

1 Cook the tortellini in a large saucepan of rapidly boiling salted water until al dente. Drain, return to the pan and keep warm.

2 Meanwhile, melt the butter in a saucepan and cook mushrooms for 2 minutes over medium heat. Add the garlic, cream, lemon zest, nutmeg and freshly ground black pepper. Stir over low heat for 1–2 minutes. Stir in the grated parmesan and cook gently for 3 minutes.

3 Add the sauce to the tortellini and stir gently to combine. Spoon into serving dishes, sprinkle with pepper and garnish with fresh herbs, if desired.

500 g (1 lb 2 oz) tortellini
60 g (2¼ oz) butter
185 g (6½ oz) button mushrooms, sliced
1 garlic clove, crushed
310 ml (10¾ fl oz/1½ cups) pouring (whipping) cream
1 small lemon, zest finely grated
pinch of freshly grated nutmeg
3 tablespoons freshly grated parmesan cheese

Chicken ravioli with balsamic dressing

»PREPARATION 25 MINUTES »COOKING TIME 5 MINUTES »SERVES 4

1 Combine the chicken, egg, orange zest, parmesan and basil in a bowl. Place a heaped tablespoon of chicken mixture in the centre of a won ton wrapper, lightly brush the edges with water and top with another wrapper. Press edges firmly together to seal. Repeat with the remaining filling and wrappers. (This is a quick way to make ravioli.)

2 Cook the ravioli in a large saucepan of rapidly boiling salted water for 5 minutes.

3 Meanwhile, combine the lime juice, vinegar, honey and oil in a small bowl and whisk to combine. Drain the ravioli and serve drizzled with the dressing and sprinkled with the chives.

250 g (9 oz) minced (ground) chicken
1 egg, lightly beaten
1 teaspoon finely grated orange zest
50 g (1¾ oz/½ cup) freshly grated parmesan cheese
1 tablespoon finely shredded basil
275 g (9¾ oz) won ton wrappers
2 tablespoons lime juice
2 tablespoons balsamic vinegar
½ teaspoon honey
1 tablespoon olive oil
finely snipped chives, to garnish

Tortellini with bacon and tomato sauce

»PREPARATION 15 MINUTES »COOKING TIME 20 MINUTES »SERVES 4

1 Cook the tortellini in a large saucepan of rapidly boiling salted water until it is al dente. Drain thoroughly and then return to pan.

2 Meanwhile, heat the oil in a medium heavy-based saucepan. Add the bacon, garlic and onion and cook for 5 minutes over medium heat, stirring often.

3 Add the chilli and tomatoes to the pan. Reduce heat and simmer for 10 minutes. Stir in the cream and basil and cook for a further 1 minute. Add the sauce to pasta and toss well. Serve immediately.

500 g (1 lb 2 oz) fresh or dried tortellini
1 tablespoon olive oil
4 bacon slices, chopped
2 garlic cloves, crushed
1 medium onion, chopped
1 teaspoon chopped red chillies
400 g (14 oz) tin chopped tomatoes
125 ml (4 fl oz/½ cup) pouring (whipping) cream
2 tablespoons chopped basil

Seafood lasagne

»PREPARATION 15 MINUTES »COOKING TIME 45 MINUTES »SERVES 4–6

1 Preheat the oven to 180°C (350°F/ Gas 4) and line a greased shallow ovenproof dish (30 cm/12 inches square) with lasagne sheets, gently breaking them to fill any gaps.

2 Slice or pull off any membrane, vein or hard white muscle from the scallops, leaving any roe attached. Peel the prawns and pull out the dark vein from each prawn back, starting from the head end. Chop the seafood into even-sized pieces.

3 Melt the butter in a large saucepan over low heat. Cook the leek over medium heat, stirring, for 1 minute, or until starting to soften. Stir in the flour and cook for 1 minute, or until pale and foaming. Remove from the heat and gradually add the combined milk and wine. Return the pan to the heat and stir over medium heat until the sauce boils and thickens.

Reduce the heat and simmer for 2 minutes. Add the seafood and simmer for 1 minute. Remove from the heat, stir in the cheddar cheese, then season.

4 Spoon half the seafood mixture over the lasagne sheets, then top with another layer of lasagne sheets. Spoon the remaining seafood over the lasagne sheets, then cover with another layer of lasagne sheets.

5 Pour the cream over the top, then sprinkle with the combined parmesan and parsley. Bake for 30 minutes, or until the lasagne is bubbling and golden brown.

250 g (9 oz) instant lasagne sheets
125 g (4½ oz) scallops
500 g (1 lb 2 oz) raw prawns (shrimp)
500 g (1 lb 2 oz) skinless firm white fish fillets (such as hake, snapper, flake, gemfish or ling)
125 g (4½ oz) butter
1 leek, thinly sliced
85 g (3 oz/⅔ cup) plain (all-purpose) flour
500 ml (17 fl oz/2 cups) milk
500 ml (17 fl oz/2 cups) dry white wine
125 g (4½ oz/1 cup) grated cheddar cheese
125 ml (4 fl oz/½ cup) cream
60 g (2¼ oz) parmesan cheese, grated
2 tablespoons chopped flat-leaf (Italian) parsley

Salmon and pasta frittata

»PREPARATION 25 MINUTES »COOKING TIME 40 MINUTES »SERVES 6

1 Add the pasta to a saucepan of boiling water and boil until al dente, then drain.

2 Put the broad beans in a bowl, cover with boiling water and leave for 10 minutes. Drain, then remove and discard the outer skins.

3 Melt the butter in a saucepan and cook the leek, stirring over medium heat until soft. Mix the pasta, broad beans, leek, salmon, egg, cream and milk in a bowl. Season to taste.

4 Pour the mixture into a lightly greased 25 cm (10 inch) frying pan. Cover and cook over low heat for 25 minutes, or until nearly set.

5 Meanwhile, heat a grill (broiler). Place the frying pan under the grill and cook until the top of the frittata has set. Set aside for 5 minutes. Cut into wedges directly from the pan. Serve with a leafy green salad.

150 g (5½ oz) spaghettini
300 g (10½ oz) frozen broad (fava) beans
30 g (1 oz) butter
1 leek, thinly sliced
415 g (14¾ oz) tinned red salmon, drained, boned and flaked
6 eggs, lightly beaten
125 ml (4 fl oz/½ cup) cream
185 ml (6 fl oz/¾ cup) milk

Pasticcio

»PREPARATION 1 HOUR »COOKING TIME 1 HOUR 50 MINUTES »SERVES 6

1 Put the flour, butter, sugar and egg yolk in a food processor with 1 tablespoon water. Process lightly until the mixture forms a ball, adding more water if necessary. Lightly knead the dough on a floured surface until smooth. Wrap in plastic wrap and refrigerate.

2 To make the filling, heat the oil in a heavy-based saucepan. Cook the onion and garlic until softened and lightly golden. Increase the heat, add the beef and cook until browned, breaking up any lumps with a fork. Add the livers, tomato, wine, stock, oregano and nutmeg, then season well. Cook the sauce over high heat until it boils, then reduce the heat, cover and simmer for 40 minutes, then cool. Stir in the parmesan.

3 To make the béchamel sauce, melt the butter in a saucepan over low heat. Add the flour and stir for 1 minute, or until the mixture is golden and smooth. Remove from the heat and gradually stir in the milk. Return to the heat and cook, stirring constantly, until the sauce boils and begins to thicken. Simmer for another minute. Season to taste.

4 Cook the pasta in a saucepan of rapidly boiling salted water until al dente. Drain and cool.

5 Preheat the oven to 160°C (315°F/ Gas 2–3) and lightly grease a 23 cm (9 inch) deep pie dish. Divide the dough in half and roll out one half to fit the base of the prepared dish, overlapping the sides. Spoon half of the meat mixture into the dish, top with the pasta and slowly spoon the béchamel over the top, allowing it to seep down and coat the bucatini. Top with the remaining meat. Roll out the remaining dough and cover the pie. Trim the edges and pinch lightly to seal. Bake the pasticcio for 50–55 minutes, or until the top is dark golden brown and crisp. Set aside for 15 minutes before cutting.

250 g (9 oz/2 cups) plain (all-purpose) flour

125 g (4½ oz) cold butter, chopped

55 g (2 oz/¼ cup) caster (superfine) sugar

1 egg yolk

150 g (5½ oz) bucatini or penne

Filling

2 tablespoons olive oil

1 onion, chopped

2 garlic cloves, finely chopped

500 g (1 lb 2 oz) minced (ground) beef

150 g (5½ oz) chicken livers

2 tomatoes, chopped

125 ml (4 fl oz/½ cup) red wine

125 ml (4 fl oz/½ cup) rich beef stock

1 tablespoon chopped oregano

¼ teaspoon freshly grated nutmeg

50 g (1¾ oz/½ cup) freshly grated parmesan cheese

Béchamel sauce

60 g (2¼ oz) butter

2 tablespoons plain (all-purpose) flour

375 ml (12 fl oz/1½ cups) cold milk

Chicken, veal and mushroom loaf

»PREPARATION 20 MINUTES »COOKING TIME 1 HOUR »SERVES 6

1 Grease a 1.5 litre (52 fl oz/6 cup) loaf tin. Cook the pappardelle in a large saucepan of rapidly boiling salted water until al dente. Drain.

2 Preheat the oven to 200°C (400°F/ Gas 6). Soak the breadcrumbs in the wine. Mix the breadcrumbs in a bowl with the chicken, veal, garlic, mushrooms, eggs, nutmeg and cayenne pepper, then season and add the sour cream, spring onion and parsley.

3 Place half the mince mixture into the prepared tin with your hands.

Form a deep trough along the entire length and fill the trough with the pappardelle. Press the remaining mince mixture over the top. Bake for 50–60 minutes, draining the excess fat and liquid from the tin twice during cooking. Cool slightly before slicing.

Note Mushrooms can be chopped in a food processor. Don't prepare too far in advance or they will discolour and darken the loaf.

100 g (3½ oz) pappardelle

20 g (¾ oz/¼ cup) fresh breadcrumbs

1 tablespoon dry white wine

375 g (13 oz) minced (ground) chicken

375 g (13 oz) minced (ground) veal

2 garlic cloves, crushed

100 g (3½ oz) button mushrooms, finely chopped

2 eggs, beaten

pinch freshly grated nutmeg

pinch cayenne pepper

60 g (2¼ oz/¼ cup) sour cream

4 spring onions (scallions), finely chopped

2 tablespoons chopped flat-leaf (Italian) parsley

Vegetable
lasagne

»PREPARATION 50 MINUTES »COOKING TIME 1 HOUR 20 MINUTES »SERVES 6–8

1 Preheat the oven to 180°C (350°F/ Gas 4). Brush a 28 x 35 cm (11¼ x 14 inch) ovenproof dish with oil.

2 Cut the capsicums in half, remove the seeds and membrane and then cut into large flattish pieces. Cook, the capsicum, skin side up, under a hot grill (broiler) for 8 minutes, or until the skin is black and blistered. Cover with a damp tea towel (dish towel) and when cool, peel away the skin and cut the flesh into long thin strips. Set aside. Chop the English spinach. Slice the mushrooms and the sun-dried tomatoes.

3 Slice the eggplant into 1 cm (½ inch) rounds and put in a large saucepan of boiling water. Cook for 1 minute, or until just tender. Drain, pat dry and set aside.

4 Heat the oil in a large heavy-based frying pan. Cook the onion, garlic and herbs over medium heat for 5 minutes, or until the onion is soft. Add the mushrooms and cook for 1 minute.

5 Add the crushed tomatoes, red kidney beans and chilli sauce and season to taste. Bring to the boil,

reduce the heat and simmer for 15 minutes, until the sauce thickens. Remove from the heat and set aside.

6 To make the cheese sauce, heat the butter in a saucepan. Add the flour and stir over medium heat for 1 minute, or until smooth. Remove from the heat and gradually stir in the milk. Return to the heat and stir constantly until the sauce boils and begins to thicken. Reduce the heat and simmer for 1 minute. Add the ricotta and stir until smooth.

7 Dip the lasagne sheets in hot water to soften slightly, if necessary. Arrange four sheets in the prepared dish. Build up layers on top of the pasta, using half the eggplant, basil, spinach, capsicum, mushroom sauce and sun-dried tomatoes. Top with a layer of lasagne sheets and press gently. Repeat the layers, finishing with a layer of lasagne. Top with the cheese sauce. Sprinkle the combined parmesan and cheddar cheeses over the sauce. Bake for 45 minutes, or until the pasta is soft.

3 large red capsicums (peppers)
500 g (1 lb 2 oz) English spinach
500 g (1 lb 2 oz) mushrooms
90 g (3¼ oz) sun-dried tomatoes
2 large eggplants (aubergines)
2 tablespoons oil
1 large onion, chopped
3 garlic cloves, crushed
1 teaspoon dried mixed herbs
1 teaspoon dried oregano
440 g (15½ oz) tinned crushed
    tomatoes
440 g (15½ oz) tinned red kidney
    beans, drained
1 tablespoon sweet chilli sauce
250 g (9 oz) packet instant lasagne
30 g (1 oz) basil leaves
25 g (1 oz/¼ cup) grated parmesan
    cheese
30 g (1 oz/¼ cup) grated cheddar
    cheese

Cheese sauce
60 g (2¼ oz) butter
30 g (1 oz/¼ cup) plain (all-purpose)
    flour
500 ml (17 fl oz/2 cups) milk
600 g (1 lb 5 oz) ricotta cheese

Baked cannelloni milanese

»PREPARATION 40 MINUTES »COOKING TIME 1 HOUR 35 MINUTES »SERVES 4

1 Preheat the oven to 180°C (350°F/Gas 4). Lightly grease a rectangular ovenproof dish.

2 In a bowl, combine the pork and veal, breadcrumbs, egg, oregano and half the parmesan, and season. Using a teaspoon, gently stuff the cannelloni tubes with the mixture. Set aside.

3 To make the tomato sauce, bring the tomato passata, crushed tomato and garlic to the boil in a saucepan. Reduce the heat and simmer for 15 minutes. Add the basil and pepper, to taste, and stir well.

4 Spoon half the tomato sauce over the base of the prepared dish. Arrange the cannelloni tubes on top and cover with the remaining sauce. Spread with the ricotta and sprinkle with the remaining parmesan and cheddar cheeses. Bake, covered with foil, for 1 hour. Uncover and bake for another 15 minutes, or until golden. Cut into squares to serve.

500 g (1 lb 2 oz) minced (ground) pork and veal
50 g (1¾ oz/½ cup) dry breadcrumbs
2 eggs, beaten
1 teaspoon dried oregano
100 g (3½ oz/1 cup) freshly grated parmesan cheese
12–15 instant cannelloni tubes
375 g (13 oz) fresh ricotta cheese
60 g (2¼ oz/½ cup) freshly grated cheddar cheese

Tomato sauce
425 ml (15 fl oz) tinned tomato passata (puréed tomatoes)
425 g (15 oz) tinned crushed tomatoes
2 garlic cloves, crushed
3 tablespoons chopped basil

EASY PASTA

Cheese and spinach cannelloni

»PREPARATION 40 MINUTES »COOKING TIME 1 HOUR 20 MINUTES »SERVES 4

1 To make the tomato sauce, heat the oil in a large pan. Add the onion and garlic and cook over medium heat until the onion is soft. Add the tomato, herbs and tomato paste and mix thoroughly. Bring to the boil, then reduce the heat and simmer for 25–30 minutes until the sauce is thick. Season to taste. Remove the bay leaves and rosemary sprigs and discard.

2 Preheat the oven to 200°C (400°F/ Gas 6). Wash and remove the stems from the spinach. Steam until just wilted. Drain thoroughly and chop

roughly. Combine the spinach with the feta, ricotta and parmesan cheeses, mint, eggs and pine nuts, and then season. Mix thoroughly. Using a small spoon or knife, carefully fill the cannelloni tubes.

3 Spoon some tomato sauce over the base of a large, shallow baking dish. Arrange cannelloni shells on top. Cover with remaining tomato sauce and mozzarella. Bake for 30–40 minutes, or until the top is golden and the pasta is tender.

Tomato sauce
2 tablespoons olive oil
1 large onion, finely chopped
2 garlic cloves, finely chopped
1.25 kg (2 lb 12 oz) tinned tomatoes,
  roughly chopped
2 rosemary sprigs
2 bay leaves
2 tablespoons tomato paste
  (concentrated purée)

500 g (1 lb 2 oz) English spinach
150 g (5½ oz) feta cheese, crumbled
150 g (5½ oz) ricotta cheese
50 g (1¾ oz/½ cup) freshly grated
  parmesan cheese
2 tablespoons finely chopped mint
2 eggs, lightly beaten
2 tablespoons pine nuts, toasted
16 instant cannelloni tubes
200 g (7 oz) mozzarella cheese,
  finely grated

Classic lasagne

»PREPARATION 40 MINUTES »COOKING TIME 1 HOUR 40 MINUTES »SERVES 8

1 Heat the oil and butter in a large heavy-based frying pan and cook the onion, carrot and celery over medium heat until softened, stirring constantly. Increase the heat, add the beef and brown well, breaking up any lumps with a fork. Add the chicken livers and cook until they change colour. Add the tomato passata, red wine and parsley, and season to taste. Bring to the boil, reduce the heat and simmer for 45 minutes, then set aside.

2 To make the béchamel sauce, melt the butter in a saucepan over low heat. Add the flour and stir for 1 minute. Remove from the heat and gradually stir in the milk. Return the pan to the heat and stir constantly until the sauce boils and begins to thicken. Reduce the heat and simmer for another minute. Add the nutmeg and season to taste. Place a piece of plastic wrap on the surface of the sauce to prevent a skin forming, and set aside.

3 Cut the lasagne sheets to fit into a deep, rectangular ovenproof dish.

4 To assemble, preheat the oven to 180°C (350°F/Gas 4). Grease the ovenproof dish. Spread a thin layer of the meat sauce over the base and follow with a thin layer of béchamel. If the béchamel has cooled and is too thick, warm it gently to make spreading easier. Place the lasagne sheets on top, gently pressing to expel any air. Continue layering, finishing with béchamel. Sprinkle with the grated parmesan and bake for 35–40 minutes, or until golden brown. Leave the lasagne to cool for 15 minutes before cutting.

Notes Instant lasagne can be used instead of fresh sheets. Follow the manufacturer's instructions. If you prefer, you can leave out the chicken livers and increase the amount of beef mince.

2 tablespoons oil
30 g (1 oz) butter
1 large onion, finely chopped
1 carrot, finely chopped
1 celery stalk, finely chopped
500 g (1 lb 2 oz) minced (ground) beef
150 g (5½ oz) chicken livers, finely chopped
250 ml (9 fl oz/1 cup) tomato passata (puréed tomatoes)
250 ml (9 fl oz/1 cup) red wine
2 tablespoons chopped flat-leaf (Italian) parsley
375 g (13 oz) fresh lasagne sheets
100 g (3½ oz/1 cup) freshly grated parmesan cheese

Béchamel sauce
60 g (2¼ oz) butter
40 g (1½ oz/⅓ cup) plain (all-purpose) flour
560 ml (19¼ fl oz/2¼ cups) milk
½ teaspoon freshly grated nutmeg

51 Gnocchi romana

49 Potato gnocchi with tomato and basil sauce

54 Parsnip gnocchi

56 Spinach and ricotta gnocchi

57 Spiced carrot and feta gnocchi

Gnocchi meals

Pumpkin gnocchi with sage butter

»PREPARATION 45 MINUTES »COOKING TIME 1 HOUR 30 MINUTES »SERVES 4

1 Preheat the oven to 160°C (315°F/ Gas 2–3). Brush a baking tray with oil or melted butter.

2 Cut the pumpkin into large pieces, leaving the skin on, and put on the tray. Bake for 1¼ hours, or until very tender. Cool slightly. Scrape the flesh from the skin, avoiding any tough or crispy parts, and transfer to a large bowl. Sift the flour into the bowl, add half the parmesan, the egg and a little ground black pepper. After mixing thoroughly, turn onto a lightly floured surface and knead for 2 minutes, or until smooth.

3 Divide the dough in half. Using floured hands, roll each half into a sausage shape about 40 cm (16 inches) long. Cut into 16 equal pieces and form each into an oval shape. Press firmly with the floured prongs of a fork to make an indentation.

4 Cook the gnocchi in batches in a large saucepan of boiling salted water for about 2 minutes, or until they rise to the surface. Drain using a slotted spoon and keep warm.

5 To make the sage butter, melt the butter in a small frying pan, remove from heat and stir in chopped sage.

6 Divide the gnocchi among serving bowls and drizzle with sage butter. Sprinkle with remaining parmesan and garnish with sage leaves.

500 g (1 lb 2 oz) pumpkin (winter squash), unpeeled

185 g (6½ oz/1½ cups) plain (all-purpose) flour

50 g (1¾ oz/½ cup) freshly grated parmesan cheese

1 egg, beaten

100 g (3½ oz) butter

2 tablespoons chopped sage, plus sage leaves, to garnish

Potato gnocchi with tomato and basil sauce

»PREPARATION 1 HOUR »COOKING TIME 50 MINUTES »SERVES 4–6

1 To make the tomato sauce, heat the oil in a large frying pan, add the onion, celery and carrot and cook for 5 minutes, stirring regularly. Add the crushed tomato and sugar and season to taste. Bring to the boil, then reduce the heat to very low and simmer for 20 minutes. Cool slightly and then process, in batches, in a food processor until smooth. Add the basil; set aside.

2 To make the gnocchi, peel the potatoes, chop roughly and steam or boil until very tender. Drain thoroughly and mash until smooth. Using a wooden spoon, stir in the butter and flour, and then beat in the eggs. Cool.

3 Turn the gnocchi mixture onto a floured surface and divide into two. Roll each into a long sausage shape. Cut into short pieces and press each piece with the back of a fork.

4 Cook the gnocchi, in batches, in a large saucepan of boiling salted water for about 2 minutes, until the gnocchi rise to the surface. Using a slotted spoon, drain the gnocchi, and transfer to serving bowls. Serve with the tomato sauce and freshly grated parmesan.

Tomato sauce
1 tablespoon oil
1 onion, chopped
1 celery stalk, chopped
2 carrots, chopped
850 g (1 lb 14 oz) tinned crushed
    tomatoes
1 teaspoon sugar
30 g (1 oz/½ cup) chopped basil

Potato gnocchi
1 kg (2 lb 4 oz) all-purpose potatoes
30 g (1 oz) butter
250 g (9 oz/2 cups) plain
    (all-purpose) flour
2 eggs, beaten

freshly grated parmesan cheese,
    to serve

Veal with peperonata and gnocchi

»PREPARATION 30 MINUTES »COOKING TIME 4–6 HOURS »SERVES 4

1 To make the peperonata, put the tomatoes in a large bowl and roughly chop with scissors. Add the remaining peperonata ingredients and mix to combine. Season with some salt and freshly ground black pepper. Add half of the peperonata to the slow cooker.

2 Put the flour in a flat dish and season well with salt and freshly ground black pepper. Trim the osso bucco pieces of excess fat and then coat the veal in the seasoned flour.

3 Heat the butter and oil in a large frying pan over medium heat, add the osso bucco and brown well for 2–3 minutes on each side. Add the wine and let it bubble and reduce a little. Arrange the veal in a single layer on top of the peperonata in the slow cooker. Pour in any juices from the frying pan, then spoon over the remaining peperonata.

4 Cook on high for 4–6 hours, or until the veal is very tender. Remove the osso bucco to a side plate, cover and keep warm. Add the gnocchi to the peperonata in the slow cooker and stir to combine. Cover and cook for a further 20 minutes, or until the gnocchi is tender.

5 To make the gremolata, combine the lemon zest, garlic and parsley in a small bowl.

6 To serve, spoon the gnocchi and peperonata onto serving plates, top with the osso bucco and sprinkle over the gremolata.

Note Use veal chops instead of veal osso bucco if you prefer.

Peperonata
400 g (14 oz) tinned whole tomatoes
1 red onion, cut into thin wedges
2 garlic cloves, chopped
1 red or green chilli, seeded and finely chopped (optional)
1 red capsicum (pepper), seeded and thinly sliced
1 yellow capsicum (pepper), seeded and thinly sliced
1 tablespoon red wine vinegar
1 teaspoon caster (superfine) sugar

60 g (2¼ oz/½ cup) plain (all-purpose) flour
4 even-sized pieces (about 750 g/ 1 lb 10 oz) veal osso bucco (see Note)
20 g (¾ oz) butter
1 tablespoon olive oil
125 ml (4 fl oz/½ cup) white wine
350 g (12 oz) packet potato gnocchi

Gremolata
grated zest of 1 lemon
1 garlic clove, finely chopped
1 large handful flat-leaf (Italian) parsley, finely chopped

Gnocchi romana

»PREPARATION 20 MINUTES + 1 HOUR CHILLING »COOKING TIME 40 MINUTES »SERVES 4

1 Line a deep Swiss roll tin (jelly roll tin) with baking paper. Put the milk and half the grated nutmeg in a saucepan and season. Bring to the boil, reduce the heat and gradually stir in the semolina. Cook, stirring occasionally, for 5–10 minutes, or until the semolina is very stiff.

2 Remove the pan from the heat, add the egg and 100 g (3½ oz/1 cup) of the parmesan. Stir to combine and then spread the mixture in the prepared tin. Refrigerate for 1 hour, or until the mixture is firm.

3 Preheat the oven to 180°C (350°F/ Gas 4) and lightly grease a shallow casserole dish. Cut the semolina into rounds using a floured 4 cm (1½ inch) cutter and arrange the rounds in the dish.

4 Pour the melted butter over the gnocchi, followed by the cream. Combine the remaining grated parmesan with the mozzarella and sprinkle on the rounds. Sprinkle with the remaining nutmeg. Bake for 20–25 minutes, or until golden.

750 ml (26 fl oz/3 cups) milk
½ teaspoon freshly grated nutmeg
85 g (3 oz/⅔ cup) semolina
1 egg, beaten
150 g (5½ oz/1½ cups) freshly grated
  parmesan cheese
60 g (2¼ oz) butter, melted
125 ml (4 fl oz/½ cup) cream
70 g (2½ oz/½ cup) freshly grated
  mozzarella cheese

Herbed potato
gnocchi with chunky tomato

»PREPARATION 1 HOUR »COOKING TIME 30 MINUTES »SERVES 4

1 To make the gnocchi, steam or boil the potato until just tender. Drain thoroughly, cool and mash. Transfer 2 cups of the potato to a large bowl. Add the egg yolk, grated parmesan and herbs and mix until combined. Gradually add enough flour to form a slightly sticky dough. Knead gently for 5 minutes, adding more flour if necessary, until smooth.

2 Divide the dough into four portions. Roll each portion on a lightly floured surface to form a sausage 2 cm (¾ inch) thick. Cut into 2.5 cm (1 inch) pieces. Roll each piece into an oval shape and roll carefully over lightly floured prongs on the back of a fork. Put on a lightly floured tray and cover until ready to use.

3 To make the sauce, heat the oil in a large frying pan, add the garlic and onion and cook over medium heat for 5 minutes, or until soft and golden.

4 Add the bacon to the pan and cook, stirring occasionally, for 5 minutes, or until the bacon is browned and crisp. Stir in sun-dried tomato, tomatoes, sugar and vinegar and bring to the boil. Reduce heat and simmer, stirring occasionally, for 15 minutes, or until the sauce has thickened. Stir the basil through the sauce or use as a garnish, if you prefer.

5 Cook the gnocchi, in batches, in a large saucepan of boiling salted water for about 2 minutes, or until they rise to the surface. Drain well and serve topped with the tomato sauce and extra parmesan.

500 g (1 lb 2 oz) floury potatoes, peeled and chopped
1 egg yolk
3 tablespoons freshly grated parmesan cheese, plus extra, for garnish
3 tablespoons chopped herbs (such as parsley, basil and chives)
125 g (4½ oz/1 cup) plain (all-purpose) flour
1 tablespoon olive oil
2 garlic cloves, crushed
1 onion, chopped
4 bacon slices, roughly chopped
150 g (5½ oz) sun-dried tomatoes, roughly chopped
400 g (14 oz) tin chopped tomatoes
1 teaspoon soft brown sugar
2 teaspoons balsamic vinegar
1 tablespoon shredded basil

Parsnip gnocchi

»PREPARATION 45 MINUTES »COOKING TIME 45 MINUTES »SERVES 4

1 Cut the parsnip into large pieces. Cook in a large saucepan of boiling water for 30 minutes, or until very tender. Drain thoroughly and leave to cool slightly.

2 Mash the parsnip in a bowl until smooth. Sift the flour into the bowl and add half the parmesan. Season and mix to form a soft dough.

3 Divide the dough in half. Using floured hands, roll each half of the dough out on a lightly floured surface into a sausage shape 2 cm (¾ inch) wide. Cut each sausage into short pieces, shape each piece into an oval and press the top gently with floured fork prongs.

4 Lower batches of gnocchi into a large saucepan of boiling salted water. Cook for about 2 minutes, or until the gnocchi rise to the surface. Use a slotted spoon to transfer to serving plates.

5 To make the garlic herb butter, combine all the ingredients in a small saucepan and cook over medium heat for 3 minutes, or until the butter is nutty brown.

6 To serve, drizzle the garlic herb butter over the gnocchi and sprinkle with remaining parmesan cheese.

500 g (1 lb 2 oz) parsnip
185 g (6½ oz/1½ cups) plain (all-purpose) flour
50 g (1¾ oz/½ cup) freshly grated parmesan cheese

Garlic herb butter
100 g (3½ oz) butter
2 garlic cloves, crushed
3 tablespoons chopped lemon thyme
1 tablespoon finely grated lime zest

Blue cheese gnocchi

»PREPARATION 20 MINUTES »COOKING TIME 20 MINUTES »SERVES 4

1 Cook potatoes in boiling salted water for 15–20 minutes or in the microwave until tender. Stir through a generous amount of salt. Drain the potatoes then mash until completely smooth. Transfer to a bowl.

2 Sprinkle the flour into the bowl with one hand while kneading it into the potato mixture with the other hand. Continue kneading until all the flour is worked in and the dough is smooth. This should take a few minutes and will be sticky at first.

3 Divide the dough into three and roll each portion into a sausage that is 2 cm (¾ inch) thick. Cut into 2.5 cm (1 inch) lengths and, using floured hands, press each gnocchi against a fork to flatten it and indent one side (indentation helps the sauce to stick to the cooked gnocchi).

4 Bring a large saucepan of water to the boil. When rapidly boiling, drop in the gnocchi, then reduce the heat and simmer until gnocchi rise to the surface. This will take 2–3 minutes. Lift the gnocchi out of the water with a slotted spoon and drain well. Keep warm on a serving dish.

5 To make the sauce put the cream in a small saucepan and bring to the boil. Boil rapidly, stirring constantly, for about 5 minutes, or until sauce has reduced by a third. Remove from the heat and stir through the cheese. Season and pour over the gnocchi. Scatter the chives over the top and serve immediately.

500 g (1 lb 2 oz) all-purpose potatoes, quartered
155 g (5½ oz/1¼ cups) plain (all-purpose) flour

Sauce
300 ml (10½ fl oz) pouring (whipping) cream
125 g (4½ oz) gorgonzola cheese, roughly chopped
2 tablespoons snipped chives

Spinach and ricotta gnocchi

» PREPARATION 45 MINUTES
» COOKING TIME 30 MINUTES »SERVES 4–6

1 Pour 125 ml (4 fl oz/½ cup) milk into a shallow dish. Remove the crust from 4 slices of white bread and soak in the milk for 10 minutes. Squeeze out all the excess liquid.

2 Squeeze the liquid from 500 g (1 lb 2 oz) thawed frozen spinach and place in a bowl with the bread, 250 g (9 oz/1 cup) ricotta cheese, 2 eggs and 50 g (1¾ oz/½ cup) of freshly grated parmesan cheese, then season. Mix thoroughly with a fork. Cover and refrigerate the mixture for 1 hour.

3 Lightly dust your hands in flour and roll heaped teaspoons of the spinach mixture into dumplings. Lower batches of the gnocchi into a large saucepan of boiling salted water. Cook for about 2 minutes, or until the gnocchi rise to the surface. Transfer to serving plates. Drizzle with melted butter and serve with parmesan shavings.

Gnocchi with fontina sauce

» PREPARATION 10 MINUTES
» COOKING TIME 15 MINUTES »SERVES 4

1 Combine 200 g (7 oz) finely chopped fontina cheese, 125 ml (4 fl oz/ ½ cup) pouring (whipping) cream, 80 g (2¾ oz) butter and 2 tablespoons grated parmesan cheese in a bowl over a saucepan of simmering water. Heat, stirring occasionally, for 6–8 minutes, or until the cheese has melted and the sauce is smooth and hot.

2 Meanwhile, cook 400 g (14 oz) fresh potato gnocchi, in batches, in a large saucepan of boiling salted water for about 2 minutes, or until they rise to the surface.

3 Drain the gnocchi using a slotted spoon and serve with the sauce poured over the top. Garnish with oregano leaves or other fresh herbs, if you like.

Potato gnocchi with tomato-olive sauce

» PREPARATION 10 MINUTES
» COOKING TIME 15 MINUTES »SERVES 4

1 Cook 500 g (1 lb 2 oz) fresh potato gnocchi in a large saucepan of rapidly boiling salted water until they float to the surface. Lift out with a slotted spoon.

2 Meanwhile, heat 2 tablespoons oil in a large saucepan and add 1 sliced leek. Stir over medium heat for 2 minutes or until tender. Add 250 ml (9 fl oz/1 cup) bottled tomato pasta sauce, 170 ml (5½ fl oz/⅔ cup) vegetable stock, 60 g (2¼ oz) chopped black olives and 6 chopped anchovies and stir for 5 minutes to heat through. Serve over gnocchi.

Storage The sauce will keep for a day, covered, in the refrigerator.

Note Fresh potato gnocchi is available from supermarkets and delicatessens. Use any other dried or fresh pasta if you prefer.

Spiced carrot and feta gnocchi

»PREPARATION 45 MINUTES »COOKING TIME 40 MINUTES »SERVES 6–8

1 Cut the carrots into large pieces and steam, boil or microwave until tender. Drain and allow to cool slightly before transferring the carrot to a food processor.

2 Process the carrot and the feta together until smooth. Transfer to a large bowl. Stir in the sifted flour, spices and egg, and mix to form a soft dough.

3 Lightly coat your fingertips with flour and shape teaspoons of the mixture into flat circles.

4 To make the minted cream sauce, melt the butter in a frying pan over medium heat, add the spring onion and garlic and cook for 3 minutes, or until the garlic is soft and golden. Add the cream, bring to the boil, then reduce the heat and simmer for 3 minutes, or until the cream has thickened slightly. Remove from the heat and stir through the mint.

5 Meanwhile, cook the gnocchi in a large pan of boiling salted water, in batches, for about 2 minutes, or until they float to the surface. Use a slotted spoon to transfer to warmed serving plates. Drizzle the minted cream sauce over the gnocchi and serve immediately.

1 kg (2 lb 4 oz) carrots
200 g (7 oz) feta cheese, crumbled
280 g (10 oz/2¼ cups) plain (all-purpose) flour
¼ teaspoon ground nutmeg
¼ teaspoon garam masala
1 egg, lightly beaten

Minted cream sauce
30 g (1 oz) butter
2 spring onions (scallions), sliced
2 garlic cloves, crushed
250 ml (9 fl oz/1 cup) cream
2 tablespoons shredded mint

63 Meatballs with fusilli

60 Penne napolitana

65 Rigatoni with tomato and haloumi

66 Rigatoni with Italian sausage

70 Rigatoni with Italian-style oxtail sauce

Short
and curly pasta meals

Penne napolitana

» PREPARATION 20 MINUTES » COOKING TIME 25 MINUTES » SERVES 4–6

1 Heat the oil in a large frying pan. Add the onion and garlic and cook for 2 minutes, or until golden. Add the carrot and celery and cook for a further 2 minutes.

2 Add the tomato and tomato paste. Simmer for 20 minutes, or until the sauce thickens, stirring occasionally. Stir in the shredded basil and season to taste.

3 While the sauce is cooking, cook the pasta in a large pan of rapidly boiling salted water until al dente. Drain well and return to the pan.

4 Add the sauce to the pasta and mix well. Serve with freshly grated parmesan cheese, if desired.

2 tablespoons olive oil
1 onion, finely chopped
2–3 garlic cloves, finely chopped
1 small carrot, finely diced
1 celery stalk, finely diced
800 g (1 lb 12 oz) tinned peeled, chopped tomatoes or
   1 kg (2 lb 4 oz) ripe tomatoes, peeled and chopped
1 tablespoon tomato paste (concentrated purée)
3 tablespoons shredded basil
500 g (1 lb 2 oz) penne
freshly grated parmesan cheese, to serve (optional)

Penne arrabbiata

»PREPARATION 30 MINUTES »COOKING TIME 50 MINUTES »SERVES 4

1 Use a large knife to finely chop the bacon fat. Chop the chillies, taking care to avoid skin irritation (wearing rubber gloves will help). Heat the olive oil in a heavy-based frying pan and add the bacon fat, chilli, onion and garlic. Cook for 8 minutes over medium heat, stirring occasionally.

2 Add the chopped tomato along with 125 ml (4 fl oz/½ cup) water and season to taste. Cover and simmer for about 40 minutes, or until the sauce is thick and rich.

3 While the sauce is cooking, cook the pasta in a large pan of rapidly boiling salted water until al dente. Drain and return to the pan.

4 Stir the chopped parsley into the sauce. Taste and season again, if necessary. Pour the sauce over the pasta and toss gently. Serve with the freshly grated parmesan or pecorino cheese sprinkled over the top, if desired.

75 g (2½ oz) bacon fat
2–3 red chillies
2 tablespoons olive oil
1 large onion, finely chopped
1 garlic clove, finely chopped
500 g (1 lb 2 oz) very ripe tomatoes, finely chopped
500 g (1 lb 2 oz) penne
2 tablespoons chopped flat-leaf (Italian) parsley
freshly grated parmesan or pecorino cheese, to serve (optional)

Macaroni cheese

» PREPARATION 25 MINUTES
» COOKING TIME 2–3 HOURS » SERVES 4–6

1 Put the pasta in a large heatproof bowl. Pour over boiling water and set aside, stirring occasionally, for 10 minutes. Drain.

2 Spray the slow cooker bowl with cooking oil spray or grease well with butter or oil.

3 Combine the evaporated milk, milk, egg and nutmeg in the slow cooker. Season with salt and freshly ground black pepper. Stir in the drained pasta, spring onion, corn, ham, 125 g (4½ oz/1 cup) of the cheddar cheese and all of the parmesan cheese. Sprinkle over the remaining cheddar.

4 Cook on low for 2–3 hours. Take care not to overcook it — the sauce will still be a little wet in the centre. If cooked for too long, it will curdle, so start checking after 2 hours — the pasta should be al dente and the sauce thick. Spoon out onto serving plates, sprinkle with the chives and serve with a salad on the side.

Orecchiette with broccoli

» PREPARATION 15 MINUTES
» COOKING TIME 25 MINUTES » SERVES 4

1 Blanch 750 g (1 lb 10 oz) broccoli florets in a large saucepan of boiling salted water for 5 minutes, or until just tender. Remove with a slotted spoon, drain well and return the water to the boil. Cook 450 g (1 lb) orecchiette pasta in the same boiling water until al dente, then drain well and return to the pan.

2 Meanwhile, heat 3 tablespoons of extra virgin olive oil in a heavy-based frying pan. Cook 8 anchovy fillets over very low heat for 1 minute. Add ½ teaspoon chilli flakes and the blanched broccoli. Increase the heat to medium and cook, stirring, for 5 minutes, or until the broccoli is well-coated and beginning to break apart. Season. Add to the pasta, add 30 g (1 oz/⅓ cup) grated pecorino or parmesan cheese and toss.

Penne with rocket

» PREPARATION 15 MINUTES
» COOKING TIME 15 MINUTES » SERVES 4

1 Roughly chop 200 g (7 oz) rocket and finely chop 3 tomatoes.

2 Cook 500 g (1 lb 2 oz) penne in a large saucepan of rapidly boiling salted water until al dente. Drain and return to the pan. Place the pan over a low heat. Add 100 g (3½ oz) butter and toss it through until it melts and coats the pasta.

3 Add the rocket and tomato to the pasta. Toss through to wilt the rocket. Stir in 45 g (1¾ oz/½ cup) freshly grated pecorino cheese and season to taste. Serve sprinkled with freshly grated parmesan cheese.

Meatballs with fusilli

»PREPARATION 35 MINUTES »COOKING TIME 35 MINUTES »SERVES 4

1 Put the meat in a large bowl and add the breadcrumbs, parmesan, onion, parsley, egg, garlic, lemon zest and juice. Season and mix well to combine. Roll tablespoons of the mixture into balls and roll the balls in the seasoned flour.

2 Heat the oil in a large frying pan and fry the meatballs until golden. Remove from the pan and drain on paper towels. Remove the excess fat and meat juices from the pan.

3 To make the sauce, in the same pan, combine the tomato passata, stock, wine, basil, garlic, salt and pepper. Bring to the boil.

4 Reduce the heat and return the meatballs to the pan. Simmer for 10–15 minutes.

5 While the meatballs and sauce are cooking, add the pasta to a large saucepan of rapidly boiling salted water and cook until al dente. Drain and serve with the meatballs and sauce over the top.

750 g (1 lb 10 oz) minced (ground) pork and veal or beef
80 g (2¾ oz/1 cup) fresh breadcrumbs
25 g (1 oz/¼ cup) freshly grated parmesan cheese
1 onion, finely chopped
2 tablespoons chopped flat-leaf (Italian) parsley
1 egg, beaten
1 garlic clove, crushed
zest and juice of ½ lemon
30 g (1 oz/¼ cup) plain (all-purpose) flour, seasoned
2 tablespoons olive oil
500 g (1 lb 2 oz) fusilli

Sauce
425 g (15 oz) tinned tomato passata (puréed tomatoes)
125 ml (4 fl oz/½ cup) beef stock
125 ml (4 fl oz/½ cup) red wine
2 tablespoons chopped basil
1 garlic clove, crushed

Ruote with lemon, olives and bacon

»PREPARATION 10 MINUTES »COOKING TIME 15 MINUTES »SERVES 4

1 Cook the ruote in a large pan of rapidly boiling salted water until al dente. Drain and return to the pan.

2 While the pasta is cooking, discard the bacon rind and cut the bacon into thin strips. Cook in a frying pan until lightly browned.

3 Combine the black olives, lemon juice, lemon zest, olive oil, chopped parsley and bacon. Gently toss the olive and bacon mixture through the pasta. Serve with freshly ground black pepper, to taste.

Note Ruote is a wheel-shaped pasta.

500 g (1 lb 2 oz) ruote (see Note)
6 bacon slices
125 g (4½ oz/1 cup) black olives, sliced
80 ml (2½ fl oz/⅓ cup) lemon juice
2 teaspoons finely grated lemon zest
80 ml (2½ fl oz/⅓ cup) olive oil
4 tablespoons chopped flat-leaf (Italian) parsley

Rigatoni with tomato and haloumi

»PREPARATION 30 MINUTES »COOKING TIME 1 HOUR »SERVES 6

1 Preheat the oven to 180°C (350°F/ Gas 4). Cut the tomatoes in half and put on a non-stick baking tray, lined with foil if you like, and sprinkle generously with sugar, salt, pepper and the garlic. Bake for 1 hour, or until quite dehydrated and shrunken. Leave to cool. Cut in half again.

2 While the tomatoes are cooking, cook the pasta in a large saucepan of rapidly boiling salted water until al dente. Drain, then rinse under cold water and drain again. Allow to cool.

3 Combine the lemon juice and olive oil and season to taste. Toss the lemon dressing through the cooked, cold pasta and lightly toss through the tomato, haloumi cheese and spinach. Serve sprinkled with freshly cracked black pepper.

6 roma (plum) tomatoes
sugar, to sprinkle
4 garlic cloves, chopped
400 g (14 oz) rigatoni
60 ml (2 fl oz/¼ cup) lemon juice
60 ml (2 fl oz/¼ cup) olive oil
200 g (7 oz) haloumi cheese, thinly sliced
100 g (3½ oz/2 cups) baby English spinach

Rigatoni with Italian sausage

» PREPARATION 15 MINUTES » COOKING TIME 20 MINUTES » SERVES 4

1 Heat a non-stick frying pan over medium–high heat. Add the sausages and cook for 5 minutes, breaking them up with a wooden spoon to crumble the meat. Add the onion and carrot and sauté for 5 minutes, or until softened. Stir in the tomatoes and garlic and reduce the heat to medium. Cook for a further 8–10 minutes, until the vegetables are tender and the mixture has thickened.

2 Meanwhile, cook the rigatoni in a large saucepan of rapidly boiling water until al dente. Drain the pasta, reserving 125 ml (4 fl oz/ ½ cup) of the cooking water.

3 Stir the drained pasta into the sauce, adding some of the reserved cooking water to thin the sauce if necessary. Season with sea salt and freshly ground black pepper.

4 Stir the rocket and olives into the pasta mixture until the leaves just wilt. Spoon into serving bowls and serve scattered with some shavings of parmesan.

300 g (10½ oz) good-quality Italian sausages, casings removed
1 onion, finely chopped
1 carrot, finely chopped
400 g (14 oz) tin chopped tomatoes
2 garlic cloves, crushed
400 g (14 oz) rigatoni
1 large handful of rocket (arugula), roughly chopped
2–3 tablespoons ligurian or other small black olives
shaved parmesan cheese, to serve

Pesto penne

»PREPARATION 25 MINUTES »COOKING TIME 20 MINUTES »SERVES 4

1 Cook the pasta in a large pan of rapidly boiling salted water until al dente. Drain well and set aside.

2 Place the pan back over medium heat. Add the olive oil and cook the tomatoes for 2–3 minutes, or until the tomatoes have softened slightly. Add the pesto, pasta, spinach leaves, basil, cream and parmesan. Cook for 3–5 minutes, or until heated through, stirring to combine well.

3 Remove from the heat, then add the garlic, pine nuts, lemon rind and bocconcini, tossing to combine well.

Season with sea salt and freshly ground black pepper and divide among warmed serving bowls. Sprinkle with the extra parmesan and serve.

Note For extra flavour, add some semi-dried (sun-blushed) tomatoes as well. For anchovy lovers, add 4 anchovies to the olive oil before frying the tomatoes — and for chilli lovers add some chilli flakes to taste. Add 150 g (5½ oz) diced salami or ham for a meat version.

500 g (1 lb 2 oz) penne
1 tablespoon extra virgin olive oil
250 g (9 oz) cherry tomatoes, halved
190 g (7 oz) jar pesto
2 large handfuls baby English
  spinach leaves
1 small handful basil, roughly chopped
60 ml (2 fl oz/¼ cup) cream
25 g (1 oz/¼ cup) grated parmesan
  cheese, plus extra, to serve
1 garlic clove, crushed
2 tablespoons pine nuts
1 teaspoon finely grated lemon rind
180 g (6 oz) bocconcini (fresh baby
  mozzarella cheese), torn

Greek lamb
with macaroni

»PREPARATION 30 MINUTES »COOKING TIME 2¼ HOURS »SERVES 4–6

1 Trim the lamb of any excess fat and cut into 3 cm (1¼ inch) cubes. Put the lamb cubes, onion, garlic, tomatoes, tomato paste, beef stock, vinegar, brown sugar and oregano in the slow cooker. Cook on high for 1 hour 45 minutes, or until the lamb is tender.

2 Place the macaroni in a large heatproof bowl, cover with boiling water and set aside for 10 minutes. Drain and add the macaroni to the slow cooker and stir to combine. Cook for a further 30 minutes, or until the pasta is tender and the liquid has been absorbed.

3 Divide among serving bowls and sprinkle with the cheese.

1 kg (2 lb 4 oz) boneless lamb leg

1 large onion, chopped

2 garlic cloves, crushed

400 g (14 oz) tinned chopped tomatoes

60 g (2¼ oz/¼ cup) tomato paste (concentrated purée)

500 ml (17 fl oz/2 cups) beef stock

2 tablespoons red wine vinegar

1 tablespoon soft brown sugar

1 teaspoon dried oregano

200 g (7 oz/2 cups) macaroni pasta

125 g (4½ oz) pecorino cheese, grated

Orecchiette with chicken sausage, tomato, rocket and parmesan

» PREPARATION 20 MINUTES » COOKING TIME 20 MINUTES » SERVES 2

1 Bring a large saucepan of salted water to the boil. Cook 180 g (7 oz/ 1½ cups) orecchiette until al dente. Drain and set aside.

2 Remove the skin from 300 g (11 oz) of chicken sausages. Heat 2 tablespoons extra virgin olive oil in a heavy-based frying pan over medium–high heat. Add the meat from the sausages and cook for 1–2 minutes, stirring to break up the meat. Reduce the heat to low, add 3 chopped anchovy fillets, 2 crushed garlic cloves and a pinch of chilli flakes (optional). Cook, stirring, for 1 minute, or until the anchovies have melted.

3 Pour in 125 ml (4 fl oz/ ½ cup) white wine and cook until it has reduced by half. Add 200 g (7 oz) halved cherry tomatoes and cook for 5 minutes, or until collapsing. Add 2 tablespoons of cream and 1 small handful of rocket (arugula) and cook for another minute, or until the cream is heated through and the rocket is wilted. Season with sea salt and freshly ground black pepper.

4 Add the orecchiette to the sauce and toss to combine well. Spoon into a serving bowl, top with shaved parmesan and serve immediately.

Rigatoni with Italian-style oxtail sauce

»PREPARATION 25 MINUTES »COOKING TIME 2 HOURS »SERVES 4

1 Heat the oil in a large heavy-based saucepan. Brown the oxtail, remove from the pan and set aside. Add the sliced onion, garlic, celery and carrot to the pan and stir for 3–4 minutes, or until the onion is lightly browned.

2 Return the oxtail to the pan, add the rosemary and red wine, cover and cook for 10 minutes, shaking the pan occasionally to prevent the meat from sticking to the bottom. Add the tomato paste and chopped tomato with 500 ml (17 fl oz/2 cups) of the stock and simmer, uncovered, for 30 minutes, stirring occasionally.

3 Add another 500 ml (17 fl oz/ 2 cups) of the stock to the pan and cook for 30 minutes. Add 250 ml (9 fl oz/1 cup) of stock and cook for 30 minutes. Finally, add the remaining stock and cook until the oxtail is tender and the meat is falling from the bone. The liquid should have reduced to produce a thick sauce.

4 Just before the meat is cooked, cook the pasta in a large saucepan of rapidly boiling salted water until al dente. Serve the meat and sauce over the hot pasta.

Note For a different flavour, you can add 250 g (9 oz) of bacon to the cooked onion, garlic and vegetables.

2 tablespoons olive oil
1.5 kg (3 lb 5 oz) oxtail, jointed
2 large onions, sliced
4 garlic cloves, chopped
2 celery stalks, sliced
2 carrots, thinly sliced
2 large rosemary sprigs
60 ml (2 fl oz/¼ cup) red wine
60 ml (2 fl oz/¼ cup) tomato paste (concentrated purée)
4 tomatoes, peeled and chopped
1.5 litres (52 fl oz/6 cups) beef stock
500 g (1 lb 2 oz) rigatoni

Casarecce with beef stew

»PREPARATION 30 MINUTES »COOKING TIME 8 HOURS 30 MINUTES »SERVES 6

1 Heat half the olive oil in a large heavy-based frying pan over high heat. Add a third of the beef and fry for 5 minutes, until golden, turning to brown all over. Transfer the beef to a slow cooker. Brown the rest of the beef in two batches, transferring each batch to the slow cooker.

2 Heat the remaining olive oil in the pan over medium–high heat. Add the onions, bacon, carrot and celery. Cook, stirring, for 5 minutes, or until the vegetables are golden. Add the garlic and cook, stirring, for a further minute.

3 Stir in the flour and cook for 1 minute, until smooth. Gradually add the tomato paste, stock, wine, thyme and bay leaves and cook, stirring, for 3 minutes, or until the

mixture boils and thickens. Pour the sauce over the beef in the slow cooker. Cover and cook on low for 8 hours, until the beef is very tender.

4 Meanwhile, near serving time, cook the pasta in a large saucepan of rapidly boiling salted water until al dente. Drain well.

5 Divide the pasta among wide, shallow serving bowls and spoon the beef mixture over the top. Sprinkle with parsley and serve with crusty bread.

2 tablespoons olive oil

1 kg (2 lb 4 oz) beef chuck steak, cut into 3–4 cm (1¼–1½ inch) chunks

8 pickling onions, about 400 g (14 oz) in total, peeled and halved

150 g (5½ oz) bacon, cut into 1.5 cm (½ inch) pieces

1 carrot, peeled and chopped

1 celery stalk, chopped into 1.5 cm (½ inch) lengths

2 garlic cloves, crushed

1½ tablespoons plain (all-purpose) flour

1 tablespoon tomato paste (concentrated purée)

125 ml (4 fl oz/½ cup) good-quality beef stock

300 ml (10½ fl oz) red wine

1 tablespoon chopped thyme

2 bay leaves

400 g (14 oz) short pasta, such as casarecce or fusilli

1 small handful chopped flat-leaf (Italian) parsley

crusty bread, to serve

Osso bucco
alla milanese

» PREPARATION 30 MINUTES » COOKING TIME 1 HOUR 40 MINUTES » SERVES 4

1 Dust the veal shank pieces with seasoned flour. Heat the oil, butter, garlic, onion and celery in a heavy-based frying pan or saucepan that is big enough to hold the shanks in a single layer. Cook for 5 minutes over low heat until softened but not browned. Add the shanks to the pan and cook for 12–15 minutes, until well browned all over. Arrange the shanks in the pan, standing them up in a single layer. Pour in the white wine and add the bay leaf, allspice and cinnamon. Bring to the boil and cover the pan. Turn the heat down to low.

2 Cook the veal at a low simmer for 15 minutes, then add 125 ml (4 fl oz/½ cup) warm water. Cook, covered, for 45–60 minutes (the timing will depend on the age of the veal), until the meat is tender and you can cut it with a fork.

Check the volume of liquid once or twice during cooking time and add more warm water as needed.

3 To make the gremolata, combine the lemon zest, parsley and garlic.

4 Transfer the veal to a plate and keep warm. Discard the bay leaf. Increase the heat under the pan and stir for 1–2 minutes until the sauce has thickened, scraping up any bits off the bottom of the pan as you stir. Season and return the veal to the sauce. Heat through, then stir in half the gremolata. Serve the veal sprinkled with the remaining gremolata.

12 pieces veal shank, about 4 cm (1½ inch) thick
plain (all-purpose) flour, seasoned, for dusting
60 ml (2 fl oz/¼ cup) olive oil
60 g (2¼ oz) butter
1 garlic clove, finely chopped
1 onion, finely chopped
1 celery stalk, finely chopped
250 ml (9 fl oz/1 cup) dry white wine
1 bay leaf or lemon leaf
pinch ground allspice
pinch ground cinnamon

Gremolata
2 teaspoons grated lemon zest
2 tablespoons finely chopped flat-leaf (Italian) parsley
1 garlic clove, finely chopped

77 **Spaghettini with garlic and chilli**

76 **Fettucine with mushroom sauce**

79 **Spaghetti with sardines**

86 Spaghetti with garlic mussels

91 Mushroom and spinach lasagne

Long
pasta meals

Fettucine with mushroom sauce

»PREPARATION 20 MINUTES »COOKING TIME 20 MINUTES »SERVES 4

1 Cook the fettucine in a large saucepan of rapidly boiling salted water until al dente. Drain, return to the pan and keep warm.

2 Cut the sun-dried tomatoes and beans into thin strips.

3 Heat the oil in a large heavy-based frying pan over medium heat. Add the onion and garlic and cook for 3 minutes, or until softened. Add the mushrooms and cook, stirring, for 1 minute. Add the wine, cream and stock. Bring to the boil, then reduce the heat and simmer for 10 minutes.

4 Lightly beat the egg in a small bowl. Stirring constantly, add a little of the cooking liquid. Pour the egg mixture slowly into the pan, stirring constantly for 30 seconds. Keep the heat low because if the mixture boils, it will curdle.

5 Add the beans, basil, pine nuts and sun-dried tomato and stir until heated through. Season to taste.

6 Serve the sauce over the pasta. Garnish with the parmesan shavings and sprigs of fresh herbs, if desired.

Note Toast the pine nuts in a dry frying pan over medium heat, stirring constantly, until they are golden brown and fragrant. Watch carefully as they will burn easily.

280 g (10 oz) fettucine

35 g (1¼ oz/¼ cup) sun-dried tomatoes

250 g (9 oz) green beans, trimmed

2 tablespoons oil

1 onion, chopped

2 garlic cloves, crushed

250 g (9 oz) mushrooms, thinly sliced

125 ml (4 fl oz/½ cup) white wine

310 ml (10¾ oz/1¼ cups) cream

125 ml (4 fl oz/½ cup) vegetable stock

1 egg

3 tablespoons chopped basil

100 g (3½ oz/⅔ cup) pine nuts, toasted (see Note)

50 g (1¾ oz) shaved parmesan cheese

herb sprigs, to serve (optional)

Tagliatelle with chicken livers

»PREPARATION 15 MINUTES
»COOKING TIME 15 MINUTES »SERVES 4–6

1 Cook 375 g (13 oz) tagliatelle in a large saucepan of rapidly boiling salted water until al dente. Drain and return to the pan.

2 Trim any discoloured parts from 300 g (10½ oz) chicken livers, then slice them.

3 Heat 2 tablespoons olive oil in a large frying pan over low heat. Cook 1 finely chopped onion and 1 crushed garlic clove until the onion is tender.

4 Add the chicken liver to the pan and cook gently for 2–3 minutes. Remove from the heat and stir in 250 ml (9fl oz/1 cup) cream, 1 tablespoon chopped chives and 1 teaspoon wholegrain mustard. Return to the heat and bring to the boil. Add 2 beaten eggs; stir quickly to combine. Remove from the heat. Add the sauce to the hot pasta and toss to combine. Serve with grated parmesan and chopped chives.

Spaghettini with garlic and chilli

»PREPARATION 10 MINUTES
»COOKING TIME 20 MINUTES »SERVES 4–6

1 Cook 500 g (1 lb 2 oz) spaghettini pasta in a large saucepan of rapidly boiling salted water until al dente. Drain and return to the pan.

2 Meanwhile, heat 125 ml (4 fl oz/ ½ cup) of extra virgin olive oil in a large frying pan. Add 1–2 seeded and finely chopped red chillies and 2–3 finely chopped garlic cloves. Cook the chilli and garlic over very low heat for 2–3 minutes, until the garlic is golden. Take care not to burn the garlic or chilli as this will make the sauce bitter.

3 Toss 3 tablespoons of chopped flat-leaf (Italian) parsley and the warm oil, garlic and chilli mixture through the pasta. Season and serve with grated parmesan cheese.

Linguine pesto

»PREPARATION 15 MINUTES
»COOKING TIME 15 MINUTES »SERVES 4–6

1 Process 100 g (3½ oz) of basil, 2 crushed garlic cloves and 40 g (1½ oz/¼ cup) toasted pine nuts in a food processor. With the motor running, add 185 ml (6 fl oz/¾ cup) of olive oil in a steady stream until mixed to a smooth paste. Transfer to a bowl, stir in 50 g (1¾ oz/½ cup) freshly grated parmesan cheese and season to taste.

2 Cook 500 g (1 lb 2 oz) linguine pasta in a large saucepan of rapidly boiling salted water until al dente. Drain and return to the pan. Toss enough of the pesto through the pasta to coat it well. Serve sprinkled with grated parmesan.

Tagliatelle with veal and cream

»PREPARATION 15 MINUTES »COOKING TIME 20 MINUTES »SERVES 4

1 Coat the veal strips with the seasoned flour. Melt the butter in a frying pan. Add the veal strips and fry quickly until browned. Remove with a slotted spoon and set aside.

2 Add the onion slices to the pan and stir until soft and golden. Pour in the white wine and cook rapidly to reduce the liquid. Add the stock and cream and then season to taste. Reduce the sauce again, and add the veal towards the end.

3 Meanwhile, cook the tagliatelle in a large saucepan of rapidly boiling salted water until al dente. Drain and transfer to a warm serving dish.

4 Stir the parmesan through the sauce. Pour the sauce over the hot pasta. Serve with extra parmesan, and garnish with flat-leaf parsley.

500 g (1 lb 2 oz) veal scaloppine or escalopes, cut into thin strips

plain (all-purpose) flour, seasoned

60 g (2¼ oz) butter

1 onion, sliced

125 ml (4 fl oz/½ cup) dry white wine

60 ml (2 fl oz/¼ cup) beef stock or chicken stock

170 ml (5½ fl oz/⅔ cup) cream

600 g (1 lb 5 oz) fresh plain or spinach tagliatelle (or a mixture of both)

1 tablespoon freshly grated parmesan cheese, plus extra, to serve

flat-leaf (Italian) parsley, to garnish

Spaghetti with sardines

»PREPARATION 30 MINUTES   »COOKING TIME 45 MINUTES   »SERVES 4–6

1 Score a cross in the base of each tomato. Plunge the tomatoes in boiling water for 10 seconds, then plunge them into cold water and peel the skin away from the cross. Cut the tomatoes in half and scoop out the seeds. Roughly chop the tomato flesh.

2 Heat 1 tablespoon of the oil in a large frying pan over medium heat. Add 1 of the crushed garlic cloves and the breadcrumbs and stir for about 5 minutes, until golden and crisp. Transfer to a plate.

3 Heat the remaining oil in the same pan and cook the onion, fennel and remaining garlic for 8 minutes, or until soft. Add the tomato, raisins, pine nuts and anchovies and cook for a further 3 minutes. Add the wine, tomato paste and 125 ml (4 fl oz/½ cup)

water. Simmer for 10 minutes, or until the mixture thickens slightly. Stir in the parsley and set aside.

4 Pat the sardines dry with paper towels. Cook the sardines in batches in a lightly greased frying pan over medium heat for 1 minute, or until cooked through. Take care not to overcook or they will break up.

5 Cook the spaghetti in a large saucepan of rapidly boiling salted water until al dente. Drain and return to the pan.

6 Stir the tomato sauce through the spaghetti until the spaghetti is well coated and the sauce evenly distributed. Add the warm sardines and half the breadcrumbs and toss gently to combine. Sprinkle the rest of the breadcrumbs over the top and serve immediately.

3 roma (plum) tomatoes
80 ml (2½ fl oz/⅓ cup) olive oil
3 garlic cloves, crushed
80 g (2¾ oz/1 cup) fresh white breadcrumbs
1 red onion, thinly sliced
1 fennel bulb, quartered and thinly sliced
40 g (1½ oz/¼ cup) raisins
40 g (1½ oz/¼ cup) pine nuts, toasted
4 anchovy fillets, chopped
125 ml (4 fl oz/½ cup) dry white wine
1 tablespoon tomato paste (concentrated purée)
4 tablespoons finely chopped flat-leaf (Italian) parsley
350 g (12 oz) butterflied sardine fillets
500 g (1 lb 2 oz) spaghetti

Spaghetti with leek and semi-dried tomatoes

»PREPARATION 15 MINUTES   »COOKING TIME 25 MINUTES   »SERVES 4–6

1 Add the spaghetti to a large saucepan of rapidly boiling salted water and cook according to the packet instructions until al dente, about 10 minutes. Drain well.

2 Meanwhile, melt the butter in a large frying pan over medium–low heat. Add the leek, season with sea salt and freshly ground black pepper and sauté for 5 minutes, or until softened and light golden.

3 Add the crushed garlic and cook for 2 minutes, then add the cream, orange rind and orange juice and simmer for 3–5 minutes.

4 Add the drained pasta, basil and semi-dried tomatoes, then toss well to coat the pasta with the sauce.

5 Divide the pasta among serving bowls, scatter with the parmesan and serve.

500 g (1 lb 2 oz) spaghetti
30 g (1 oz) unsalted butter
4 leeks, white part only, thinly sliced
2 garlic cloves, crushed
300 ml (10½ fl oz) cream
2½ teaspoons finely grated orange rind
80 ml (2½ fl oz/⅓ cup) orange juice
1 small handful basil, chopped
80 g (2¾ oz/½ cup) thinly sliced semi-dried (sun-blushed) tomatoes
50 g (1¾ oz/½ cup) shaved parmesan cheese

Spaghetti bolognese

»PREPARATION 25 MINUTES »COOKING TIME 1 HOUR 35 MINUTES »SERVES 4–6

1 Heat the oil in a large, heavy-based saucepan over medium heat. Reduce the heat to low, add the onion, celery and carrot and sauté for 10 minutes, or until the onion is translucent. Add the anchovies, garlic and thyme sprigs and cook for a further 1 minute, or until the anchovies have dissolved.

2 Increase the heat to high, add the minced veal and season with sea salt and freshly ground black pepper. Cook for 3–4 minutes, or until light golden, stirring with a wooden spoon to break up the meat. Add the mushrooms and cook for 1 minute.

3 Reduce the heat to medium. Add the tomato paste and cook, stirring, for 30 seconds. Add the white wine and bring to a simmer. Cook for 4 minutes, or until the liquid has reduced by half.

4 Add the tomatoes, bay leaves and 125 ml (4 fl oz/½ cup) water. Bring to the boil, then reduce the heat to medium–low, cover and simmer for 30 minutes.

5 Remove the lid and simmer for 30–40 minutes, or until the ragù is thick. Remove from the heat, stir in the basil and adjust the seasoning to taste. Discard the thyme sprigs and bay leaves.

6 When the ragù is nearly cooked, cook the spaghetti in a large pot of rapidly boiling salted water until al dente. Drain well.

7 Divide the spaghetti among four serving bowls. Spoon the ragù over the top and scatter with the shaved parmesan and extra thyme sprigs.

1½ tablespoons olive oil
1 large onion, finely chopped
1 celery stalk, finely chopped
1 carrot, finely chopped
6 anchovies, chopped
4 garlic cloves, crushed
2 thyme sprigs, plus extra, to garnish
1 kg (2 lb 4 oz) minced (ground) veal, not too lean
90 g (3¼ oz/1 cup) chopped Swiss brown mushrooms
100 g (3½ oz) tomato paste (concentrated purée)
200 ml (7 fl oz) white wine
2 x 400 g (14 oz) tins chopped tomatoes
2 bay leaves
1 small handful basil, torn
500 g (1 lb 2 oz) spaghetti
50 g (1¾ oz/½ cup) shaved parmesan cheese

Pasta with Italian sausages

» PREPARATION 20 MINUTES » COOKING TIME 25 MINUTES » SERVES 2

1 Place the oil in a frying pan over medium heat, add the onion and garlic and cook, stirring often, for 5 minutes, or until softened. Add the sausages, breaking up the meat with a wooden spoon, and cook, stirring, for 3–4 minutes or until the meat changes colour. Add the raisins, vinegar, sugar, stock, red wine and thyme to the pan.

2 Bring the mixture to the boil, then reduce the heat and cook for 10–15 minutes, stirring occasionally until the sauce is reduced.

3 Meanwhile, cook the pasta in a large saucepan of rapidly boiling salted water until al dente. Drain well, place in four serving bowls, top with the sauce and serve immediately, garnished with the thyme and shaved parmesan and the rocket salad on the side.

2 tablespoons olive oil

1 large red onion, cut into thin wedges

2 garlic cloves, crushed

3 Italian sausages (about 175 g/6 oz), skins removed

3 tablespoons raisins, chopped

2 tablespoons balsamic vinegar

2 teaspoons brown sugar

170 ml (5½ fl oz/⅔ cup) chicken or beef stock

170 ml (5½ fl oz/⅔ cup) red wine

3 teaspoons fresh thyme or 1 teaspoon dried, or to taste, plus a few sprigs to serve

200 g (7 oz) fettucine

shaved parmesan and rocket (arugula) salad, to serve

Spaghetti carbonara

» PREPARATION 10 MINUTES » COOKING TIME 20 MINUTES » SERVES 6

1 Cook the spaghetti in a large saucepan of rapidly boiling salted water until al dente. Drain and return to the pan.

2 While the spaghetti is cooking, discard the bacon rind and cut the bacon into thin strips. Cook the bacon in a heavy-based frying pan over medium heat until crisp. Drain on paper towels.

3 Beat the eggs, grated parmesan and cream in a bowl until well combined. Add the bacon and pour the sauce over the warm pasta. Toss gently until the pasta is well coated.

4 Return the pan to the heat and cook over low heat for 1 minute, or until slightly thickened. Season with freshly ground black pepper and serve garnished with chives.

500 g (1 lb 2 oz) spaghetti
8 bacon slices
4 eggs
50 g (1¾ oz/½ cup) freshly grated
    parmesan cheese
310 ml (10¾ fl oz/1¼ cups) cream
snipped chives, to garnish

Lamb meatballs
with spicy saffron sauce

»PREPARATION 30 MINUTES + 30 MINUTES CHILLING »COOKING TIME 8 HOURS 15 MINUTES »SERVES 4

1 To make the meatballs, combine the meatball ingredients in a large bowl and mix together well using your hands. Using clean wet hands, form the mixture into 24 meatballs, using one heaped tablespoon of the mixture per ball. Place the meatballs on a plate, cover and refrigerate for 30 minutes.

2 Meanwhile, to make the spicy saffron sauce, soak the saffron threads in 2 tablespoons hot water for 5 minutes to infuse.

3 Place the almonds and garlic in a food processor and pulse until a smooth paste forms. Add the ground hazelnuts, passata, vinegar, capsicum and one tin of chopped tomatoes. Process to a smooth consistency. Add the saffron water, paprika, cayenne pepper, chilli flakes and sugar and pulse until thoroughly mixed. Pour the mixture into a slow cooker with the remaining tin of chopped tomatoes.

4 Heat the oil in a frying pan over medium heat. Add the meatballs in batches and fry for 3–4 minutes each time, or until evenly browned, turning often and transferring each batch to the slow cooker. Cover and cook on low for 8 hours.

5 Meanwhile, near serving time, cook the pasta in a large pot of rapidly boiling salted water until al dente. Drain well.

6 Divide the pasta among serving bowls. Season the meatball mixture to taste with sea salt and freshly ground black pepper, then spoon the meatballs and sauce over the top. Sprinkle with parmesan and basil leaves and serve.

2 tablespoons olive oil
400 g (14 oz) fresh pappardelle
grated parmesan, to serve
basil leaves, to garnish

Meatballs

650 g (1 lb 7 oz) minced (ground) lamb
100 g (3½ oz/1 cup) dry breadcrumbs
1 egg, lightly beaten
1 garlic clove, crushed
2 teaspoons dried oregano
½ teaspoon sea salt
½ teaspoon freshly ground black pepper
2 tablespoons olive oil

Spicy saffron sauce

1 teaspoon saffron threads
115 g (4 oz/¾ cup) blanched almonds, toasted
1 garlic clove, crushed
55 g (2 oz/½ cup) ground hazelnuts
2 tablespoons tomato passata (puréed tomatoes)
2 tablespoons red wine vinegar
340 g (12 oz) jar roasted red capsicum (pepper) strips, drained
2 x 400 g (14 oz) tins chopped tomatoes
2 teaspoons paprika
1 teaspoon cayenne pepper
1 teaspoon chilli flakes
2 teaspoons soft brown sugar

Spaghetti with garlic mussels

»PREPARATION 20 MINUTES »COOKING TIME 15 MINUTES »SERVES 4

1 Cook the spaghetti in a large saucepan of rapidly boiling salted water until al dente. Drain.

2 Meanwhile, scrub the mussels with a stiff brush and pull out the hairy beards. Discard any broken mussels, or open ones that don't close when tapped on the bench. Rinse well.

3 Heat the oil in a large saucepan. Add the garlic and stir over low heat for 30 seconds. Add the wine and mussels. Simmer, covered, for 5 minutes. Remove the mussels, discarding any that don't open.

4 Add the cream and basil to the pan and season to taste. Simmer for 2 minutes, stirring. Serve the sauce and mussels over the spaghetti.

500 g (1 lb 2 oz) spaghetti
1.5 kg (3 lb 5 oz) mussels
2 tablespoons olive oil
2 garlic cloves, crushed
125 ml (4 fl oz/½ cup) dry white wine
250 ml (9 fl oz/1 cup) cream
2 tablespoons chopped basil

Veal and vegetable stew with noodles

» PREPARATION 15 MINUTES » COOKING TIME 2 HOURS » SERVES 4

1 Heat 1 tablespoon of the olive oil in a large heavy-based saucepan or flameproof casserole dish over medium heat. Add half of the veal and cook for 5 minutes, until lightly browned, turning often. Transfer to a plate. Repeat with the remaining oil and veal.

2 Add the carrot, celery, onion and garlic and sauté for 10 minutes, or until the onion is soft. Return all the veal to the pan, add the flour and stir continuously for 1 minute, until thoroughly combined.

3 Pour in the white wine and cook, stirring, for 1 minute, or until the sauce is smooth and thick. Add the tomatoes, stock, oregano, lemon rind and lemon juice and bring to the boil. Reduce the heat to low, cover and simmer for 1½ hours, or until the veal is very tender.

4 When the veal is nearly ready, add the tagliatelle to a large pot of rapidly boiling salted water and cook until al dente. Drain well.

5 Toss the melted butter through the tagliatelle. Divide the tagliatelle and veal among four serving plates. Sprinkle with the parsley and serve.

2 tablespoons olive oil
1 kg (2 lb 4 oz) veal shoulder, cut into 3 cm (1¼ inch) chunks
2 carrots, diced
2 celery stalks, sliced
2 small onions, diced
2 garlic cloves, crushed
1½ tablespoons plain (all-purpose) flour
250 ml (9 fl oz/1 cup) white wine
400 g (14 oz) tin chopped tomatoes
125 ml (4 fl oz/½ cup) chicken stock
1 teaspoon dried oregano
finely grated rind and juice of 1 lemon
450 g (1 lb) fresh tagliatelle
40 g (1½ oz) butter, melted
1 large handful flat-leaf (Italian) parsley, roughly chopped

Bacon, pea and walnut carbonara

» PREPARATION 15 MINUTES
» COOKING TIME 15 MINUTES » SERVES 4–6

1 Cook 500 g (1 lb 2 oz) spaghetti in a large pan of rapidly boiling salted water until al dente.

2 Meanwhile, cut 4 slices of bacon into thin strips. Heat 1 tablespoon olive oil in a frying pan. Cook the bacon for 5 minutes, until slightly crisp. Add 3 finely chopped garlic cloves and 155 g (5½ oz/1 cup) thawed frozen peas. Sauté over low heat for 3 minutes, then set aside.

3 Whisk 4 eggs, 75 g (2½ oz/¾ cup) grated parmesan cheese and 185 ml (6 fl oz/¾ cup) cream, and season.

4 Drain the spaghetti, return to the pan and toss over low heat for 2 minutes. Toss the bacon and peas through, then add the egg mixture. Stir for 1–2 minutes, taking care not to let the mixture boil. Remove from the heat, cover and stand for 2–3 minutes, until thickened. Toss 90 g (3¼ oz/¾ cup) of chopped toasted walnuts through the pasta. Serve with parsley and parmesan.

Linguine with almond pesto

» PREPARATION 15 MINUTES
» COOKING TIME 20 MINUTES » SERVES 4

1 Preheat the oven to 180°C (350°F/ Gas 4). Roast 60 g (2¼ oz/⅓ cup) blanched almonds for 4–5 minutes, or until lightly toasted. Cool, then finely chop in a food processor with 1 sliced garlic clove. Blend with 25 g (1 oz) mint leaves, 1 small handful flat-leaf (Italian) parsley and 125 ml (4 fl oz/½ cup) olive oil until well combined. Add 50 g (1¾ oz/½ cup) grated pecorino cheese and pulse until just combined. Season to taste.

2 Cook 3 diced all-purpose potatoes in a large saucepan of boiling salted water for 10 minutes. Add 200 g (7 oz) chopped green beans and cook for 3 minutes, or until the vegetables are tender. Drain well.

3 Cook 400 g (14 oz) linguine in a saucepan of boiling salted water until al dente. Drain well, reserving 2 tablespoons of the water. Return the pasta to the pan with the water. Toss with the potato, beans and pesto. Serve with grated pecorino.

Fettucine with zucchini

» PREPARATION 15 MINUTES
» COOKING TIME 15 MINUTES » SERVES 6

1 Heat 250 ml (9 fl oz/1 cup) olive oil in a small frying pan and cook a handful of basil leaves, two leaves at a time, for 1 minute, or until crisp. Remove with a slotted spoon and drain on paper towel.

2 Cook 500 g (1 lb 2 oz) fettucine in a large pan of rapidly boiling salted water until al dente. Drain and return to the pan.

3 While the fettucine is cooking, grate 500 g (1 lb 2 oz) of zucchini (courgettes). Heat 60 g (2¼ oz) butter in a deep saucepan over low heat until the butter is foaming. Add 2 crushed garlic cloves and cook for 1 minute. Add the grated zucchini and cook, stirring occasionally, for 1–2 minutes or until softened. Add to the hot pasta, along with 75 g (2¾ oz/¾ cup) grated parmesan cheese and toss well. Serve the pasta garnished with the crisp basil leaves.

Creamy beef with cherry tomatoes and sun-dried tomatoes

»PREPARATION 20 MINUTES »COOKING TIME 6 HOURS 30 MINUTES »SERVES 4–6

1 Place the flour, salt, pepper and paprika in a large bowl. Add the beef and toss until evenly coated. Shake off any excess flour, then place the beef in a slow cooker.

2 Mix the tomato paste and wine, then add to the beef with the onion, garlic, cherry tomatoes and semi-dried tomatoes. Gently mix together. Clean the sides of the bowl with a damp cloth if necessary. Cover and cook on low for 5–6 hours, or until the beef is very tender.

3 Stir in the sour cream, then cover and cook for another 30 minutes, or until heated through.

4 Meanwhile, close to serving time, cook the pasta in a large saucepan of rapidly boiling salted water until al dente. Drain well.

5 Divide the pasta among serving bowls, then spoon the beef mixture over the top. Sprinkle with the pine nuts, scatter the basil leaves and parmesan over the top and serve.

35 g (1¼ oz/¼ cup) plain (all-purpose) flour

2 teaspoons sea salt

½ teaspoon freshly ground black pepper

1 teaspoon sweet paprika

1.5 kg (3 lb 5 oz) beef chuck steak, trimmed of fat, then cut into 3 cm (1¼ inch) chunks

1½ tablespoons tomato paste (concentrated purée)

60 ml (2 fl oz/¼ cup) white wine

1 onion, finely chopped

2 garlic cloves, crushed

500 g (1 lb 2 oz) cherry tomatoes, halved

90 g (3¼ oz/½ cup) semi-dried (sun-blushed) tomatoes, chopped

250 g (9 oz/1 cup) sour cream

400 g (14 oz) fresh pappardelle

toasted pine nuts, for sprinkling

small basil leaves, to garnish

shaved parmesan, to serve

Fettucine with roast fennel, saffron, olives and breadcrumbs

»PREPARATION 15 MINUTES + 30 MINUTES SOAKING »COOKING TIME 45 MINUTES »SERVES 4

1 Preheat the oven to 180°C (350°F/Gas 4). Put the saffron in a small bowl, pour in the wine and leave to soak for 30 minutes.

2 Place the fennel, onion and garlic in a baking dish. Drizzle with 80 ml (2½ fl oz/⅓ cup) of the olive oil and toss to coat. Bake for 45 minutes, or until the fennel is golden and tender.

3 Reduce the oven to 120°C (235°F/Gas ½). Add the saffron and wine to the fennel and onion mixture, then return to the oven to keep warm.

4 Meanwhile, pulse the bread in a food processor until coarse crumbs form. Heat the remaining olive oil in a heavy-based frying pan and stir the breadcrumbs over medium–low heat for 5–6 minutes, or until crisp and golden. Drain on paper towels and set aside.

5 Bring a large saucepan of salted water to the boil. Add the fettucine and cook for 3–4 minutes, or until al dente. Drain well, then return the pasta to the saucepan.

6 Add the fennel mixture to the pasta with the olives, pine nuts, herbs, rocket and breadcrumbs. Toss well to combine.

7 Divide the pasta among serving bowls and serve scattered with parmesan shavings if desired.

a large pinch of saffron threads
60 ml (2 fl oz/¼ cup) white wine
4 fennel bulbs, trimmed, tough cores removed, then thinly sliced
2 red onions, halved and thinly sliced
4 garlic cloves, finely chopped
125 ml (4 fl oz/½ cup) olive oil
80 g (2¾ oz) day-old sourdough bread, crusts removed
500 g (1 lb 2 oz) fresh fettucine
80 g (2¾ oz/½ cup) pitted kalamata olives, sliced
40 g (1½ oz/¼ cup) toasted pine nuts
1½ tablespoons chopped oregano
3 tablespoons chopped flat-leaf (Italian) parsley
1 small handful baby rocket (arugula)
shaved parmesan cheese, to serve (optional)

Mushroom and spinach lasagne

» PREPARATION 30 MINUTES » COOKING TIME 30 MINUTES » SERVES 4

1 Heat oil and butter in a large non-stick frying pan over medium–high heat. Sauté the portobello, Swiss brown, and oyster mushrooms for 5 minutes, or until browned and softened. Add enoki mushrooms, baby spinach and garlic and cook for 1 minute. Stir in verjuice and stock and bring to the boil, then reduce heat to low and stir in crème fraîche, gorgonzola and marjoram. Simmer over medium heat for 1 minute, until reduced to a light sauce consistency. Season to taste with salt and ground black pepper.

2 Bring two large saucepans of salted water to the boil. Cut each sheet of lasagne into three even squares or rectangles. Cook in the boiling water for 3–4 minutes, or until al dente. Drain.

3 Place a lasagne sheet portion on each serving plate. Spoon one-third of the mushroom mixture over the top. Add another lasagne portion to each and top with another third of the mushroom mixture. Arrange the remaining lasagne portions over the top and spoon over the remaining mushroom mixture.

4 Sprinkle with the hazelnuts, garnish with the extra marjoram and serve.

60 ml (2 fl oz/¼ cup) olive oil
60 g (2¼ oz) unsalted butter
300 g (10½ oz) large portobello or field mushrooms, thinly sliced
200 g (7 oz) Swiss brown mushrooms, thickly sliced
100 g (3½ oz) oyster mushrooms
150 g (5½ oz) shimeji or enoki mushrooms, separated
200 g (7 oz) baby English spinach leaves
3 garlic cloves, crushed
100 ml (3½ fl oz) verjuice
100 ml (3½ fl oz) vegetable stock
200 g (7 oz) crème fraîche or sour cream
100 g (3½ oz) gorgonzola cheese, crumbled
1 small handful marjoram, plus extra, to garnish
4 fresh lasagne sheets
30 g (1 oz/¼ cup) chopped roasted hazelnuts

Beef in red wine and chocolate on pappardelle

»PREPARATION 30 MINUTES »COOKING TIME 3 HOURS 15 MINUTES »SERVES 4–6

1 Preheat the oven to 170°C (325°F/Gas 3). Season the beef with sea salt and ground white pepper.

2 Heat 1 tablespoon of the olive oil in a large flameproof casserole dish over high heat. Cook the beef in batches for 4–5 minutes, or until browned all over, turning often and adding a little more oil as necessary. Remove each batch to a plate.

3 Heat the remaining oil in the dish over medium heat. Add the onion, celery and garlic and sauté for 10 minutes. Add the wine and boil for 5 minutes, or until it has reduced by half.

4 Return all the beef to the dish, along with the prunes, cinnamon sticks, rosemary sprigs, tomatoes and stock. Bring just to a simmer, then cover with a tight-fitting lid or a double layer of foil and transfer to the oven. Bake for 1½–2 hours, or until the beef is tender.

5 Remove the dish from the oven. If necessary, place some paper towel on the surface of the sauce to absorb any excess oil.

6 Using a slotted spoon, remove the beef from the sauce to a warm plate and cover with foil. Set aside while finishing the sauce.

7 Simmer the sauce remaining in the casserole dish over high heat for 20 minutes, or until reduced by half, stirring often. Return the beef to the casserole and allow to heat through. Add the chocolate, then stir until the chocolate has melted and the mixture is smooth.

8 Spoon the beef over bowls of cooked pappardelle pasta. Garnish with extra rosemary, grated orange rind and parmesan and serve with crusty bread.

2 kg (4 lb 8 oz) beef chuck steak, cut into 5 cm (2 inch) chunks
80 ml (2½ fl oz/⅓ cup) extra virgin olive oil
3 onions, chopped
2 celery stalks, chopped
6 garlic cloves, thinly sliced
450 ml (16 fl oz) red wine
330 g (11½ oz/1½ cups) pitted prunes, chopped
2 cinnamon sticks
2 rosemary sprigs, plus extra chopped rosemary, to garnish
2 x 400 g (14 oz) tins chopped tomatoes
750 ml (26 fl oz/3 cups) beef stock
50 g (1¾ oz/⅓ cup) chopped good-quality dark chocolate (70 per cent cocoa)
500 g (1 lb 2 oz) cooked fresh pappardelle pasta
finely grated rind of 1 orange
grated parmesan, to serve
crusty bread, to serve

Index

EASY PASTA

Published in 2011 by Murdoch Books Pty Limited.

Murdoch Books Australia
Pier 8/9, 23 Hickson Road, Millers Point NSW 2000
Phone: +61 (0)2 8220 2000 Fax: +61 (0)2 8220 2558
www.murdochbooks.com.au

Murdoch Books UK Limited
Erico House, 6th Floor North, 93–99 Upper Richmond Road
Putney, London SW15 2TG
Phone: + 44 (0) 20 8785 5995 Fax: + 44 (0) 20 8785 5985
www.murdochbooks.co.uk

Publisher Lynn Lewis
Design Concept Adam Walker
Designer Lena Lowe
Editor Justine Harding
Project Manager Liz Malcolm
Production Alexandra Gonzalez

National Library of Australia Cataloguing-in-Publication Data:
Title: Easy Pasta: a classic kitchen collection for the busy cook.
ISBN: 978-1-74266-421-7 (pbk.)
Series: MB test kitchen favourites.
Notes: Includes index.
Subjects: Cooking (Pasta).
Dewey Number: 641.822

Printed by C & C Offset Printing Co. Ltd, China